JOE GILBERT

Base Camp to Boardroom

A Mountaineer's Guide To Business Success

Copyright © 2024 by Joe Gilbert

All rights reserved. No part of this publication may be reproduced, stored or transmitted in any form or by any means, electronic, mechanical, photocopying, recording, scanning, or otherwise without written permission from the publisher. It is illegal to copy this book, post it to a website, or distribute it by any other means without permission.

First edition

This book was professionally typeset on Reedsy.
Find out more at reedsy.com

Contents

1	Foreword	1
2	Introduction	2
3	Know your destination	5
4	It starts with action	9
5	Watch out for the spiders	13
6	Use your BRAIN	18
7	What could go wrong?	23
8	Learn to let go	27
9	Aim for the stars	33
10	The power of how	37
11	Leave your comfort zone	42
12	Practice Gratitude	50
13	Find your why	56
14	The importance of showing up	63
15	Learn when to walk away	67
16	Pain Vs Discomfort	73
17	Climbing is better with friends	80
18	Invest in the right tools	84
19	If you can't change your environment, change your mindset	89
20	Slow and steady wins the race	96
21	The Importance of Going at Your Own Pace	102
22	The Art Of Delegation: The Power of a Well-Organised Team	108
23	The Twists and Turns on the Path to the Summit	115

24	Great communication makes for a great leader	121
25	A picture speaks a thousand words	127
26	Keep to the path	132
27	Type Two Fun	136
28	Take in the views	139
29	Energy is key	142
30	Into the fog	147
31	Final Thoughts	151

1

Foreword

Climbing the mountain can never get easier. You can only get stronger.

~ Joe Gilbert

This book is dedicated to Jo Sahunta, my coach and mentor. Your guidance has been a compass in the fog and a light in the dark.

Thank you for believing in me, even when I failed to believe in myself.

2

Introduction

Hi, I'm Joe - business owner and avid mountaineer. These are my two great passions in life, and over the years I have learnt many amazing lessons from my time in the mountains that have translated very well into business.

When you're in the mountains, you're dealing with extreme survival conditions and life or death situations. You need strong leadership, snap decision making, comprehensive planning, and the ability to stay calm and focused under pressure.

These skills are also critical in business, and yet I see so many business owners who don't have these skills and their businesses struggle as a result.

When climbing a mountain, success is clearly defined. You don't "successfully nearly summit" – you either summit or you don't. In business it's not so black and white; many business owners never take the time to define what success looks like, and as a result spend their lives struggling but convincing themselves that because they're keeping

INTRODUCTION

their head above water they're successful.

What I love most about the mountains is they offer unparalleled time and opportunity to reflect and think things through. No phone signal, no social media, no emails, no fires to fight, no problems to deal with or "urgents" that get in the way of focus. Just you and your two feet walking through nature, for hours or days or even weeks at a time, uninterrupted.

I do some of my best thinking in the mountains, and often come back with an intense clarity and exquisitely simple solutions to what I thought were highly complex problems. It's true that sometimes you can't see the wood through the trees – at high altitude there are no trees, just you and your thoughts.

This book does not offer ideas or theory, but rather a practical step-by-step guide and action plan to overcoming some of the most common problems business owners face, based on the lessons I've learned climbing mountains all around the world. I'm by no means a business guru that has all the answers. But I have learned a lot of lessons, made a lot of mistakes, and spent years figuring things out that I wish I'd known from the start.

Finally, the mountains have taught me that up high, your problems down below seem insignificant. When you're hanging off an exposed ridge at 5,000m racing to get to shelter before a storm hits with the wind lashing your face, suddenly that rude customer who complained the other day doesn't seem like much of a problem at all anymore.

Being in a risky situation staring death in the face, you wonder why you ever let yourself get so stressed by the minor things that didn't matter in the scheme of things, but seemed like a big deal at the time.

Have fun and remember to enjoy the journey!

~ Joe

Descending Aiguille du Midi, France

3

Know your destination

When people set out to climb a mountain, they have a pretty clear vision. "I want to climb [insert mountain name here]." Can you imagine how the conversation would go if a friend told you their plan to vaguely climb some mountains?

"So what are you up to this weekend Joe?"

"Oh, I'm just off to climb some mountains."

"Cool! Which ones?"

"Not sure. I'll just drive around until I find some and then start climbing."

"But how will you know which direction to head in? And how do you know what equipment to bring? Or how much food to take? Or whether you'll need a tent?"

"No idea. I'll figure it out along the way I guess."

You'd probably think your friend was pretty stupid, and try to talk them out of having such a foolish plan. Once you've picked which mountain you want to climb, planning becomes easy. You'll be able to quickly work out how to get there, where to park, what equipment you need, how long it will take, what food and provisions you'll need, whether you need to book accommodation etc. And of course, once you're there, you'll know how to find your way up to the top – either following a path, following a map, or hiring a guide.

If you never knew where you were going, how could you ever get there? You'd never find your way to anything, and would inevitably end up giving up and coming home after a day's wandering around seeking a destination that you'd never set.

When I have a destination set, I'll know exactly how to get there, what supplies and equipment to bring, what clothes to pack, whether I'll need to book accommodation or not, which route I'm taking, and how much time to book off work. If I didn't know where I was going, how could I have any of that prepared?

In Business

Setting off into the mountains without a destination or vision of where you want to get to seems idiotic. So why is it, again and again, business owners go wandering off into the marketplace with absolutely no idea where they're heading, how they are going to get there, or what they want from their business? How could you possibly know which products and services to develop, which USPs to push, what value you're adding to the market, and what tools you need to get there, if you don't know where you're going? How could you ever achieve success if you don't know what success looks like?

And yet, I see this ALL THE TIME in business! So many clients come to us wanting digital marketing services, and when I ask what their goals are from the campaign, so many answer "We're not sure, just more customers."

"How many more? How can you know if the campaign has been successful if you don't know what success looks like? How can we advise you on an appropriate ad-spend if we don't know how many clients you are looking to take on?"

I encourage all business owners to stop wandering blindly through the market with no idea where they're headed, and pick a destination! It doesn't need to be perfect or wildly ambitious, and it's fine for your vision to change over time, but you do need to have a vision for what your completed business looks like.

Action Points

1. Write a vision of what you want your business to deliver on a personal level, i.e. "I want an income of £XX.XX per month from this business, and to not have to work more than three days per week." Be specific, don't go writing something vague like "I want to work less hours than I do currently and I want lots of money."

2. Write a list of bullet points about how your company will look when it's finished, including specific figures and numbers, e.g. My business will turnover £XX.XX p/m, My profit margins will be 50%, I will have a team of 5 including an operations manager, 2 x technicians, a marketing manager, and a support operator, My business will be fully systemised and can run without me in it.

3. Write your overall vision of what your business will bring to the table. This is critically important; if your business brings nothing to the table and is just a clone of every other business in your sector, what's the point of existing? You could be cheaper, better, higher-quality, more luxury, faster, more personal, offer a new way of operating, or you could find a way of completely disrupting the market. What you mustn't be is the same as everybody else.

Snowdon Summit with friends

4

It starts with action

Want to know the reason I've successfully summited more mountains than anyone I know? Trust me, it's got nothing to do with skill, natural mountain climbing ability or an extreme level of fitness! The reason I've summited so many mountains is simple: I've picked a destination, put on my boots, and climbed. In other words, I took action.

The first mountain I ever climbed was Ben Nevis in Scotland. I didn't spend a long time researching options, I didn't wait to assemble a team, I didn't hang around waiting for perfect weather conditions, and I didn't have any special equipment. I just bought myself some mountain boots, drove across to the start of the walk near Fort William, and started climbing. I had nothing more than a bottle of water and a bar of chocolate with me. And you know what? It was fantastic! One of the loveliest climbs I have ever done. Perfection is the enemy of inaction, and too often people wait so long for all the "ducks to align" that they never get started in the first place.

Taking action first and figuring out how I'll make everything work second has lead me to booking spectacular hikes and climbs around the world. Taking action was what lead me to walk out of my dead-end job and start my own business. Taking action lead me to picking up a laptop and starting work on this book.

If no one ever took any real action, and only ever sat dreaming about the things they'd like to do, no one would ever do anything!

In Business

Far too often I see business owners fail to take the action that's necessary to hit their goals. Whether that is hiring a new member of staff, launching a new product or service, going-live on a marketing campaign, investing in that new piece of equipment, hiring a business coach, or calling that prospect back.

Without taking massive action, businesses will never get massive results. Too many businesses fall into the trap of relying on a "hope for the best" strategy. They fail to truly take the action that's needed, and hope that things will one day just get better, they'll get lucky, the winds will change, or the market will improve.

It's often the case that companies will just about get by and crawl along without ever really innovating or doing anything radical, which is fine... until a well-funded competitor with ambitious growth plans comes along, takes massive action, and blows them out of the water.

I saw this happen with my Dad's business. For years he had been a local market leader in the private tuition sector. However, he neglected the evolving marketing sphere, continuing to advertise in Yellow Pages as he always had done. Year on year business got quieter, but instead of taking the action needed, he carried on ploughing money into Yellow

Pages and hoping things would go back to how they were. Of course, they did not, and one day a big American company with a substantial online marketing presence and a fancy online digital system swooped in and put him out of business.

Had my Dad of taken the action necessary to get online and dominate the Google rankings when he had the chance, he could have had a thriving business by the time the American company came into play, and enough money to properly rival them.

Action points

1. Write a list of five actions you need to take TODAY to improve things around the office. This could be small such as "upgrade the coffee machine to improve staff satisfaction," or "Get into work 30 minutes earlier," or it could be bigger such as "call three marketing agencies and invite them in to quote for promoting our new product or service." Don't let this stage overwhelm you... it's fine for action to start small. Just don't do nothing.

2. Write a list of five actions you need to stop doing, TODAY! We need to free up time for some new activity and growth. Usually it's the small things that hold us back, like procrastinating, replying to WhatsApp's during work, answering emails all day, or micromanaging / undertaking tasks you really should be delegating.

This is the exact strategy I use, both in business and when preparing for an upcoming trek. I'll identify things I need to start doing such as exercising each morning, eating veg with each meal, upping my protein intake, or reducing carbs. I'll identify things I need to stop doing, like drinking beer, eating ice cream, or driving to work everyday when I could cycle twice a week.

In business I try to do this exercise quarterly in order to avoid bad habits sneaking in. It's amazing how much rubbish you can clear from your life by writing a "stop doing" list, and how much headspace you'll free up for positive action!

My first ever mountain summit, Ben Nevis, Scotland

5

Watch out for the spiders

Something was wrong. As I struggled to open my eyes and drag myself from sleep, I could feel something was wrong, but my sleepy brain wasn't sure what yet. We were camping not far from Banff in the Canadian Rockies, and it was the tenth day of a 14 day trip.

As I sleepily sat up and tried to move, I realised it was my left arm that was causing my grievance. It felt heavy and swollen and sore and intensely itchy all at the same time. I lifted it into view and was shocked to see that my arm had literally swollen to twice its size! It was red and swollen and bloated and for a second I contemplated cutting it off with my Swiss Army knife to alleviate the relentless itching.

Closer inspection in the light showed two little red puncture marks in the skin; the tell-tale signs of a spider bite.

Thankfully some anti-histamines and antibiotic cream brought my arm back down to a normal size relatively quickly, and it didn't get any worse than that. But it reminded me of an instance where I was stung on the hand by an unidentified little black flying thing in the foothills of the

Swiss Alps, which brought on an intense red-hot searing pain like I have never felt in my life; if I hadn't of seen it happen I would have thought someone had stabbed me with a blade.

It got me thinking about how curious it is that of all the animals and creatures that I've been around on my expeditions, it's always the smallest ones that cause the most pain. I've trekked through placed populated by bears, wolves, mountain lions, snow leopards, cougars and snakes, yet somehow the only thing that's ever caused me harm is the tiny little bugs that you'd least expect to be a threat.

In Business

In business, funnily enough it is also those smallest clients that cause you the most pain - every time! You know, the ones that drive down a hard bargain at the start, insisting they only want something simple. You know you shouldn't, but you want to help them out and they seem like nice guys, so you drop your rates and make an exception.

And of course, they are always, without fail, the ones who cause you the most pain! They pick and criticise every little detail, want to change everything, never make up their minds, are the first to moan and complain about "how disappointed" they are, are needy and demanding, rude, and of course completely ungrateful that they got a massive discount in the first place.

My nice nature has lead me to getting stung like this more times than I can count in business. When you have a big client and the project slips outside of scope a little, you can quote them a few £thousand extra and they're cool with it. But the little clients, eugh - quote them another £50 for something and all hell breaks loose.

The only times I have ever had clients yelling down the phone at me, sending me long angry emails, telling me how disappointing they are with the service, and throwing their toys out the pram, are the times I've taken on what should be a small simple project and given a discount. Sure, bigger clients can be demanding too - but at least they've paid for that privilege.

In the early days of running my business, it was very very hard to turn down work, even when I knew I should. When you know that £3k client is going to cause trouble, but you need to put food on the table and have no other clients, what do you do? You suck it up and get bitten.

I remember this one client I had in my first year of running my marketing agency; he was paying me £150 a month for me to regularly update his website with new content. These days I wouldn't bat an eyelid at £150 p/m, we have clients paying us £5,000+ p/m, but back then I was dependent on it - that measly £150 p/m meant I could buy food each month. But this guy was the worst kind of horrible - picking up the phone and screaming at me, threatening, sending emails late at night demanding things, just generally being a bully. Finally one day I'd had enough, and mid-rant I interrupted him and said *"Dean - we're done. Find another agency."* And with that I hung up the phone and never spoke to him again. What a lovely, liberating day that was. And you know what, 9 years later we're still here doing just fine without his £150!

I've had other clients pay us similar amounts for web support, only to raise tickets literally 2-3 times daily and constantly irritating the team. Anyone like that is now let go of if things don't improve after a stern warning (*my favourite is when you give them a warning and they respond with "we'll take our business elsewhere!" and you're thinking "sir... please do."*)

Thankfully as we've grown, we've got to a point where we can afford to turn down clients if we want to, and fire the bad ones. It's so true that 80% of your problems come from 20% of your clients.

Firing bad clients is honestly the best thing you can do for your business. Running a business is one of the hardest things you can do in life, and it's stressful enough without bad clients. Don't add to that stress and struggle by having difficult clients. Trust me, get rid of the spiders in your business, you're better off without them.

Action Points

1. Make a list of your clients , and include how much they're paying you.

2. Now rank each client out of 10, with 1 being a "horrible awful causes you loads of pain" client and 10 being a "golden wonderful love working with them" client.

3. For anyone ranked under five, have a look and see if there's any patterns or common denominators. Are they paying less? Are they from a certain industry or sector?

4. If you've got anyone who's a 1 or 2, I'd urge you to consider dropping them. Really think about what your business could do without them? It could give you time and head space for a bigger, better client who pays more and doesn't cause you pain. Or you'd come home less stressed each night.

5. Now that you know who is causing you pain, make a list of warnings for future clients likely to cause pain; I literally have a saved listed

called "no go list." If someone like that comes knocking, turn them down. I know it's not easy when you need money, but be brave and do it. You'll thank yourself for it in the long run!

Don't let the spiders ruin your hardwork and get you down. Get rid of them, and go catch something more profitable ;)

6

Use your BRAIN

Sometimes when hiking in the mountains, there is a need to make quick, calculated decisions. Decisions that are life-or-death. There is no time to dawdle, you have limited information by which to make your decision, but making the wrong one could prove fatal. This is how it is when you're spending time in extreme hostile environments, and a mountaineer must be able to quickly choose from the best of a bad choice of options, and choose fast.

A great example of this was when I was hiking in the alps with a couple of friends once. Our path involved crossing a steep rocky pass, which should have been a straightforward route. However, when we got to the pass, a combination of extremely heavy snowfall in winter and a hotter than usual spring had turned the rocky pass into a fast-flowing torrent. Oh, and a storm was heading in our direction and the light was fading...

We had three options:

1. Cross the torrent, where a slip would almost certainly be fatal.

2. Head back to the hut where we came from, which would be a 7 hour trek and leave us out after-dark in freezing conditions and exposed to the storm.

3. Try and go around the torrent, which could add 5-6 hours onto our journey, and we had no guarantee that the pass was any better further up. The devil you know vs the devil you don't!

So, what to do? Cross the torrent and risk death, or go around / head back which meant exposure to life-threatening conditions? It's easy to panic in these situations, which of course would have done nothing to help our dilemma. But make the wrong decision and it could have been game over for all of us.

In these situations, I think it's important to remove fear and emotion from the decision, and to come to the best possible logical decision. So for rapid logical decision making, I use the BRAIN method. This stands for:

- BENEFITS – what are the benefits of taking this action?
- RISKS – what are the risks of this action?
- ALTERNATIVES – if we don't take this action, what else can we do?
- INSTINCT – what does my gut tell me?
- NOTHING – what happens if we don't do anything at all?

Let's run the above situation through our BRAIN model:

- **BENEFITS** – what are the benefits of crossing the torrent?
- Will arrive at our destination in under an hour where we will have safety and shelter from the storm and be indoors before nightfall.
- We know what we're dealing with – other routes could be worse.

- **RISKS** – what are the risks of this action?
- We could slip and fall to our deaths.

- **ALTERNATIVES** – if we don't take this action, what else can we do?
- Trek 5 - 6 hours to the next pass point, which could be either better or worse.
- Trek 7 hours back to the hut we came from, leaving us exposed to the elements and no guarantee of spaces at the hut.

- **INSTINCT** – what does my gut tell me?
- Gut says we can do this; we can cross that damn torrent! It probably looks worse than it is, no sign of slippery moss, and if we work as a team and rope up we can minimise risk. Being stuck out here in the storm after dark could be treacherous for the entire group.

- **NOTHING** – what happens if we don't do anything at all?
- Not an option – we have to keep moving.

After running the problem through the BRAIN model and eliminating emotion, I came to the logical conclusion that crossing the torrent was the option that presented the least risk and dealt with the least unknowns. So we went for it.

We roped up together, and sent the tallest guy (who was somewhat of a giant!) with the longest legs across first (who was quite easily able to leap over the entire thing!) Once the giant was safely across, I went next; as the lightest member of the team my two friends were able to act as anchors were I to slip, and hopefully they should be able to haul me back up. (I did actually slip, but thankfully my friends' anchoring held strong, and the worst I got was a wet boot!) Finally the third guy and heaviest of the group went last, using the combined weight of the Giant and I to safely hold his weight.

All three of us made it safely across the pass, and less than an hour later were safely making ourselves comfortable in our lodge enjoying a hot bowl of soup watching the blizzard slowly close in outside.

In Business

The need for rapid but sensible, logical decisions devoid of emotion is critical in business.

"Do I hire that new marketing person? Shall I move forward with this opportunity that's presented itself? Shall I accept this client who is asking for more than we can currently deliver?"

As business owners, we have to make these decisions all the time, sometimes with limited information or insights. It's usually not quite as life-critical as when you're in the mountains, but having a system for logical decision making is still helpful.

I regularly run business queries through the BRAIN model, as well as encouraging my team to do the same in order to develop their problem-solving abilities.

Action Points

Write down the BRAIN model (Benefits, Risks, Alternatives, Instinct, Nothing) on a business card, and put it in your wallet (or just save it on your phone, if you're modern.) Next time you have to make any sort of decision about anything, even something mundane like whether you should book a certain hotel or which car to buy, give it a go.

The BRAIN model has honestly changed my life, and helped me to make a lot of sensible decisions under pressure without letting emotion clog my thought. Give it a go, and hopefully it will work well for you too

How to cross safely? Decisions decisions... French Alps

7

What could go wrong?

Before heading off into the mountains, I always like to make a quick list of what could go wrong, accompanied by what I can do to solve that problem should it occur. Rugby Coach Sir Clive Woodward famously phrases this as "Thinking correctly under pressure," or "T-CUP Moments."

Of course this will change for each mountain, depending on things like terrain, length of trip, or how remote we're going to be. But when we're dealing with hostile environments and possible survival situations, being equipped and ready to rapidly deal with a variety of problems in the mountains where there's little help around can be the difference between life and death.

We can't think of everything, nor can we prepare for every eventuality, otherwise we'd be carrying far too much kit. So typically on a hike I ask myself, "What are the top ten things that could go wrong on this trip? I then write a list of these points, with solutions to each of these problems.

For example:

- Water bottle could leak / get dropped and roll off a cliff. Solution: Bring 2 x 1L water bottles instead of 1 x 2L water bottle. Ensure they're leakproof.
- Sole of boots could come away. Solution: Bring Duct-tape
- It could rain. Solution: Bring waterproofs and dry bag for phone
- I could get stuck in a ravine and have to saw off my own arm (*This actually happened to a climber called Aron Ralston, made famous by the film 127 Hours*). Solution: bring very sharp Swiss army knife with saw attachment.
- Minor surface wounds. Solution: carry first aid kit
- Deep cut. Solution: carry bandage roll
- Aches / pains / sprains: Solution: Carry Ibuprofen
- Get lost and stranded: carry survival bag, torch, whistle and fire making kit

When you're a long way from civilisation, nipping into your local shop or pharmacy isn't an option. The only tools you have for survival are those you carry with you on your own back.

In Business

A few years ago, I decided to adopt this methodology into my business. Not only were we spending a lot of time fire-fighting, but it was impossible for me to ever take real time away from the business, as my team didn't know how to deal with the issues we were facing. So, exactly like I did with the mountains, I wrote a "TCUP Moments" list for the business.

This included absolutely every single problem I could think of, and how to solve that problem. Things such as what happened if the batteries to the keyboard died (*amazingly this is the sort of mundane thing I was*

WHAT COULD GO WRONG?

spending all day dealing with as a Managing Director!), what to do if a client was late paying, what to do if a member of staff handed in their notice, what happened if the office was closed, what if an employee's payslip is wrong, what if a client was unhappy and demanding a refund, what if someone threatened legal action against us, what if a client's website got hacked etc etc.

This list is available for the entire team to view, and every time an issue arises, no matter how minor, we write down the solution and add it to the list. This means that even new employees with no experience can solve these issues on their own.

Alas, no more constant fire-fighting, no more turning to the MD for every little problem.

Just like my backpack in the mountains, my business T-CUP list also included a range of new tools and resources to enable my team to solve issues without me there. This includes things like cost calculators in case a client wants changes, decision-making flowcharts on whether a client should be charged for a revision, email templates for a whole range of issues, quote generators in case a prospect is after a new quote, and flow-charts in case a client has a complaint.

Action Points

- Write down your own list of T-CUP moments for your business. List absolutely everything that could go wrong, no matter how silly or rare you think it is. Think back to past issues you've had before, and how they are best solved.

- Go as far as to write scripts and email templates that your team can use to handle customer issues. Include important phone numbers and key contacts so that your team know who to call in your absence.

- Finally, write a list of "Only You" problems, meaning only you can solve them. If you ever want a holiday without being constantly disturbed with issues, find a way that others can also solve these issues.

Lots to go wrong when you're ice-climbing in the Atlas Mountains!

8

Learn to let go

"Joe, let go! You have to let go!"

"I can't!"

"You can, I've got you, let go!"

It was a cold, blustery day up in the North Welsh mountains. I was on a climbing course, and my instructor and I were about 900m up a vertical cliff face. I'd got to a point where I was well and truly stuck; I couldn't reach the nearest hand-hold above me, and I'd made a complex manoeuvre to get to where I was which meant I couldn't backtrack or go anywhere else.

I glanced down nervously at the ground hundreds of metres below me. I was shaking, felt sick with fear, my muscles were growing weak with fatigue, the cold wet wind ripped through me, and I was hanging on for dear life. I was literally frozen in fear.

My only option was to either make a leap of faith and jump for the handhold above me which was about a foot out of my reach, or to stay there until I eventually gave up on life and let go.

In reality I was in no real danger; I was attached to my instructor by rope, he had a good hold, and he'd secured his end of the rope to a large boulder above me. The worst case scenario was I'd come off the cliff, the rope would (hopefully) stop me plummeting to my death, and my instructor would hoist me up. But my fear of heights can be crippling, and in that instance the fear overtook the logic.

"You have to let go mate. Trust me, I've got you. Just jump, you can make it. And if you don't you're roped up, you'll be fine."

"I can't do it!"

"You have to! You can't stay here."

"Can't we get a helicopter or something?"

"No! Now fucking jump!"

So I let out a deep breath, swore, and jumped. I caught the handhold by the tips of my fingers and hoisted myself up, to where I was able to get into a good position and complete the rest of the climb with no problem. Taking that leap was one of the scariest things I've ever done. I remember nearly passing out from both stress and relief and exhaustion when I'd made it. If I hadn't of taken a leap of faith and let go, I might never have been able to complete the climb.

In Business

On the drive home from that trip, I thought long and hard about my learnings in the Welsh mountains. It occurred to me that had I not have let go of the ledge and taken a leap of faith, I would hypothetically still be stuck up there in the same place, without making it to the top. I had to adopt a new way of thinking, putting my trust in something beyond my own hands (the rope and the instructor.)

I started to think about what I needed to let go of in my business, and what new heights I could reach if I put my trust in others and adopted new ways of thinking. I concluded that if I wanted to leave my current position and grow the business to new heights, I would have to let go of being in full control. I needed to put the right people in the right positions, then get out of the way.

It became clear to me that if I remained in charge of design, operations, sales, marketing, finance, HR, customer service, IT, and purchasing, then I would quickly become the bottle neck in the business. It would never grow beyond my own skill sets, capabilities or availability. The extent of the businesses' growth would be limited to me – and I am only one little man. In other words, I would be adding a very low ceiling to the success of my company.

"Joe let go. You have to let go!"

I started to think about what steps I'd need to take in order to let go. First, I let go of the low skilled, low fun jobs – things that were easy to delegate and that I wouldn't miss doing, such as reconciling invoices and writing contracts. I hired additional staff to run the everyday things such as support and basic revisions; it made no sense for me as a business owner to be helping customers reset their password or making very basic web edits such as making a font bigger or changing an image.

Next I promoted my administrator to Operations Managers. She was super organised, I was all over the place. It was crazy that I was literally forgetting to invoice people or set up direct debits because I was too busy fighting fires or out networking.

Then I promoted my senior web designer to head of design. I made it clear that this was his department, all responsibility and design issues would fall under his remit. It was up to him to let me know where the shortages were, where further training was needed, what software we were lacking, and when / who we needed to hire.

Next I hired a marketing manager; our marketing was being constantly neglected, because I was too busy dealing with the problems I had to go and generate new ones. Perhaps on some level I didn't want to get busier, and was subconsciously stunting our own growth. If I continued to be in charge of marketing, we'd never get further than the handful of clients who were either recommended to us or found their way to us through some other channels.

Finally I hired a few technicians to help with things like reporting and account management, content creation, PPC management, and SEO. This didn't happen overnight of course; this team I built up over 7 years. But I started with drawing up the company structure of where I wanted to be, and slowly slowly I made it happen. Now my job is doing what I do best; developing the business, coming up with ideas, and helping my team achieve their full potential.

Actions

In order to grow your business, you need to let go.

1. Firstly, list everything that you do. Absolutely everything.
2. Next come up with a list of things in your business you can let go of right away, with minimal training or supervision. If you don't have a team, think about things you can easily outsource like social media, IT, content creation, accounts and bookkeeping, marketing, or admin support.
3. Then figure out what is taking up most of your time, and which of these things you could either let go of in time, or partially let go of but still supervise.
4. Finally start creating systems and guides on how to do the things that you do, or only you know how to do.

For years I thought I was the only one who could do certain things. I didn't trust others to do it properly, and thought that unless I did it, it would get done wrong. Once I started writing systems, I realised I didn't have to trust others to think how I thought; I just needed to trust my own system that I'd created and teach others how to follow it.

Take project pricing for example. For years I was the only one who could price up projects. I thought I had some gut intuition on how to cost things based on all my years in the trade, and knowing how big a project would be. But then I sat and wrote up the sort-of-process that I went through in my head. This included things like "how many hours will this project take? Do we know this to be a difficult client who typically complicates everything? Will I need to buy in any plugins or resources to achieve this? Is this a big client with big resources or a cash strapped client where every penny counts?"

I built a nice calculator that anyone on the team could follow. The only real estimation was the amount of hours the job would take, but it was built with plenty of tolerance for error included. Once all the fields were filled out, the calculator would spit out a figure for the job. I tested it over and over, and each time it would spit out a pretty accurate figure inline with what I would have "plucked out of thin air." I had essentially cloned a small part of myself, the part that decides how much to charge for work. It also helped because, unlike me, the calculator didn't have days where it either felt generous or felt mean, so our jobs were priced consistently.

9

Aim for the stars

I remember the first time I climbed Ben Nevis, the highest mountain in the UK at 1,345m. For many people this is a brilliant achievement, perhaps even the achievement of a lifetime. Many are anxious about taking on such a climb, and worried about whether they will succeed. But for me it was practice.

I don't mean that it any sort of an arrogant way; in just a few months I was to be taking on Mt Ebnehfluh in Switzerland, which sits at just under 4,000m above sea level. I knew I must get as fit as possible for this climb, which meant climbing as many mountains as possible in the lead up to it. So I set off to Fort William in Scotland, parked up at the base of Ben Nevis, and up I went.

Now even though Ben Nevis was at that time the highest mountain I had ever climbed, I never saw it as a challenge. In my head it was simply a milestone that must be reached before moving on to the "real challenge."

I won't say the climb was easy, but I certainly never found it difficult.

In my head whenever I started to get a little tired, I'd say to myself "Ah come on this is nothing. You'll be climbing double this height in a few months! Stop whining and get on with it!"

My mindset had shifted from "Will I be able to summit Ben Nevis?" to "how quickly can I summit Ben Nevis?" This resounding optimism meant that there was never a doubt in my mind, and failure wasn't an option. This meant that every time the whiney little protective voice in my head woke up and tried to tell me I couldn't do this, I was easily able to shut it off and say "Shut up brain, this is nothing! Go back to sleep!"

There is a classic saying in life which is "aim for the stars, and even though you may not hit them, you may land on the moon." This saying couldn't be truer in mountaineering. Even though Ben Nevis was never my goal and was simply a warmup for me, by aiming high I'd still completed a fantastic achievement in summitting the UK's highest peak.

In Business

This lesson is one of the most prominent teachings in business growth I have ever encountered. Far too often I see business owners aim too low, and this mindset stunts growth and limits effort. For example, imagine your business goals were to increase revenue by 5% over the next 12 months. But a downturn in the economy means things are quieter than expected, and you only hit 2.5% growth. Ok, that's still growth, right?

But imagine now if you had aimed to grow by 50% over the next 12 months. You applied all the tools and techniques needed to achieve such a massive growth, faced the same economic downturn, and only hit 25% growth. I say only, 25% growth in 12 months is still MASSIVE, right?

What I'm getting at here is whatever your goal is, times it by ten. You'll apply a totally different set of tools and techniques than if you'd aimed for your original goal. You'd be looking at things like aggressive marketing campaigns, acquisitions and mergers, new product launches etc. All things that you'd unlikely consider if you simply aimed for the original goal. Grant Cardone talks a lot about this in his book "The 10x Rule" – which says that you should set targets for yourself that are 10X greater than what you believe you can achieve, and you should take actions that are 10X greater than what you think are necessary to achieve your goals. The biggest mistake most people make in life is not setting goals high enough. Setting massive goals and taking massive action is the only way to fulfil your true potential and get massive success.

However, I do believe that it is critical that you believe it can be done. How could you possibly put in 10X effort into hitting a 10X goal that you never believed was possible? You'd quit at the first hurdle, telling yourself "I knew this idea was silly and a waste of time, it's not possible."

The first motor car, the first plane, the first rocket, the first brain surgery... would any of these things ever have been attempted if the visionaries behind these things didn't believe they were possible? Optimism is essential in business, and without it you'll be battling your own self-doubts every step of the way.

Action Points

1. Whatever your goals are (and by now you really should have goals written down), re-visit them and ask yourself "what would this goal look like if it was ten times bigger?

2. Now ask yourself what strategies and tools you'd need to achieve

your new goal?

3. You may struggle to believe in your new goal, so take a minute to say "what precedents exist for this goal? Has anyone else in my industry achieved this? Have other business owners in other industries achieved something similar?" This can help reassure you that your goal is possible.

4. Now go make your plan!

Final push to the summit of Mt M'Goun, Morocco

10

The power of how

"How" is one of my favourite words in the dictionary. I believe it is one of the most powerful words we have, and when we learn to use it, we learn to really utilise our brain's problem solving potential.

Let me explain...

It was October 2012, and I'd just booked onto a trek across the Bernese Oberland in the Swiss Alps which looked fantastic! It promised breathtaking vistas, challenging climbs, and a foray into winter skills which would require ropes, crampons and ice axes. In true impulsive-Joe style, I booked first and asked questions later.

However, once the initial excitement of having just booked the most challenging mountaineering trip to date wore off, those questions sure did come rolling in! I'll be honest, I started freaking out a little bit. "You don't have the skills to do this trip. What if you're not fit enough? Where are you even going to get the money to pay for it? You don't have any of the necessary equipment!"

"Ok Joe, get a grip" I said to myself, "panicking is not going to get you up those mountains and back. Think strategically about this!"

So I did. I wrote down a list of everything that was making me nervous, and then I simply added "How" to the beginning of each question.

- "How can I afford to pay for this?"
- "How can I get fit enough to successfully complete this expedition?"
- "How can I get my hands on all the equipment I need?"
- "How can I ensure I have all the skills necessary to avoid dying on this trek?"

See when you ask yourself "HOW" can I solve this problem, instead of just stating "I have a problem," you start utilising a whole new set of areas of your brain to find a solution. When you're in panic mode or are anxious about a problem, generally your Amygdala is in control. The Amygdala is the part of your brain responsible for processing emotions, especially fear and anxiety, and really isn't the best when it comes to problem solving. If you're freaking out about a problem, like "OMG I'm not fit enough for this trek!" and you put your Amygdala in control, you'll really struggle to come up with sensible solutions.

However, when you rephrase your anxiety as a question, you're essentially saying "Hey brain, it's problem solving time! I need your help with something." Brain says "No worries! Amygdala, go to sleep we don't need you right now. Prefrontal Cortex, wake up! You are the area responsible for executive functions, such as planning, decision-making, and problem-solving. Temporal Lobes, you're in charge of memory retrieval. We could do with you on this also. Parietal Lobes, you're responsible for the attention and integration of information. You might help combine various pieces of knowledge relevant to the question. Anterior Cingulate Cortex – you're responsible for error detection, conflict monitoring, and deciding between potential options. You can help us evaluate different strategies or pathways to address the question."

So you see, when you turn a negative statement such as "I'm not fit enough for this climb!" to a question such as "How can I get fit enough for this climb?" you engage much more of your brain that just the little Amygdala which does not have the same problem solving capabilities as its colleagues!

By tackling my concerns in this approach, I was able to come up with plenty of sensible solutions to solve all of my questions. For example, I followed a fitness training plan designed for Mont Blanc; I knew this would be overkill for my trip, which should ensure I should be more than fit enough by the time it came to the climb. I also phoned a local hire shop and managed to secure a good price on hiring all the equipment I'd need which saved me a lot of money over purchasing it. I phoned some old contacts and managed to land a handful of freelance bits of work that pretty much paid for everything. And I had a good chat with the tour operator who reassured me that all the skills I'd need would be taught on the trip, and my previous experience in the mountains was plenty. Oh, and I successfully completed the expedition with no issues whatsoever.

In Business

Too often in my line of work, I see business owners operating from a place of panic. "The economy is down right now! We're dangerously close to running out of capital! Our competitor just invested heavily in a marketing campaign! Our systems have just gone down!"

As we have learned, operating from a place of panic does not yield effective decision making results. Business owners should rephrase their anxieties into questions phrased in a positive manner.

- "Some companies do seriously well in a recession! How can we be one of them?"
- "How can we turn an economic downturn to our advantage?"
- "How can we quickly raise more funds?"
- "How can we blow our competitor's fancy marketing campaign out of the water and make them look silly?"
- "How can we get our systems up and running, mitigate damage control, and make improvements to ensure this doesn't happen again?"

I find using this approach also helps my staff think differently. If a campaign isn't performing or I feel a website design could be improved, rather than saying "this campaign isn't performing, what's wrong with it?" (which usually triggers an excuse or a temptation to somehow blame the client) or "hmm I'm not loving this design, go re-do it" (which is demoralising and hurtful) I'll say "Hey guys, I noticed this campaign isn't performing very well this month. How can we improve conversions?"

Instead of making excuses or getting their guard up, I'm getting the team to use their brains to come up with solutions to a specific problem rather than just getting defensive or feeling they have to somehow get out of trouble.

Action Points

Write a list of everything that's concerning you around your business right now. Even if it's only something small, like "Our office is a bit cluttered" or "my staff seem to be taking more sick days than I'd imagine."

Now rephrase all of these issues into "How statements." "How can we make our office tidy, bright and a pleasant working environment?" "How can I design a well-being programme to boost employee health?"

Once you have your list and have come up with solutions to each question, go implement your solutions. I like to re-visit this exercise at the end of every month, to stop little issues creeping up on me! I want the question to be "How can we get our turnover back up to where it was last month?" rather than "How can we avoid impending bankruptcy!"

11

Leave your comfort zone

Let me tell you about the single most challenging, difficult thing I have ever done; the toughest climb of my life and the furthest from my comfort zone I think I have ever been. It was January 2017, 4am, and we were about to leave our hut for the summit attempt of Mt Toubkal in Morocco – the tallest mountain in North Africa at 4,167m. And I was struggling.

A series of events had lead me to be in a position where I really was not in a good shape to climb that mountain. In true impulsive-Joe style, I'd booked the trip just six weeks in advance; not nearly enough time to properly commit to any sort of training plan or get myself in good shape. Being just after Christmas / New Year, I'd inevitably eaten too much food and drunk too much alcohol, just to add to my overall lack of mountain-readiness. The week before I flew out I'd had a rotten cold/cough/flu thing that had knocked me for six! I was over it by the time I left the UK, but it left me weak and tired. I'd also strained my knee (*the dodgy one with the torn ligament and no cartilage*) carrying the Christmas tree down from the loft and missing the bottom rung of the ladder, meaning I landed on it quite hard and it was aching bad. In all honesty I should never have been on that mountain, but I was young and naïve and these trips aren't cheap, and I didn't think carrying some excess Christmas weight was a valid reason for my insurance company to pay out if I cancelled.

Leading up to summit day, I was exhausted following three nights of no sleep. I was unprepared for the freezing temperatures that the huts would drop down to at night high up in the Atlas mountains, and my sleeping bag was not adequate to keep me warm. So for three nights I had laid awake shivering and uncomfortable and regretting my terrible life choices, wondering why I was here in this stupid freezing hut with no heating in my stupid inadequate sleeping bag.

By the morning of summit day, the altitude was really starting to get to me. I felt sick to my stomach, I couldn't eat any breakfast, and I'd barely touched my dinner.

So yeah, I was a mess. By the time that 4am alarm went off on summit morning, I was already up and pacing around the cabin trying not to throw up following another sleepless night and struggling with a pounding headache. Should I have gone for that summit attempt? No. Was I safe and in a good position to attempt it? Probably not. Was I about to let my weak tired body hold me back and get in the way of achieving my dreams, and quit? Not a chance! I knew that having gotten so far and so close, I couldn't just quit without even trying. Every fibre of my body was screaming at me to give this one a miss, to take it easy and chill at the cabin with some hot tea and soup, that the mountain would be there to climb another day. But I knew that I would feel like a total failure if I hadn't of at least tried to make the climb.

So I began. I started the now familiar routine of layering up, lacing my boots, checking my kit and ensuring I knew exactly where everything was in my bag, strapped on my head-torch, clipped on my crampons, put on my gloves, picked up my ice axe, and stepped outside into the freezing arctic conditions to breathe in the fresh night air.

"You ok?" asked the guide.

"Yep!" I replied.

"You not look ok" he said.

Once everyone was ready, we began. Roped up together and walking in single file, we slowly began the long, steep climb towards the summit – due to take us around 5 -6 hours if things went to plan. We climb at night when it's coldest because that's when the snow is frozen solid and safest to walk on. When it starts getting hot in the day, you're at risk of avalanches.

We were ascending quickly due to the sharp incline of the mountain, and with each step the air became thinner. I felt sicker and sicker with each step I took, and breathing became increasingly harder. I couldn't walk more than a few steps before I'd have to stop and catch my breath.

As we got higher, the winds picked up force and were howling all around us, slashing our faces with frozen snow that feels a lot like getting slapped with sand paper. I'd tried to tie a buff around my face, but it didn't stand a chance against the strong wind and was instantly torn off.

Every step became harder and harder, but on and on we trudged, one step after another, slowly inching our way closer and closer to the summit.

I was battling with my mind... my brain was trying it's best to protect me by screaming "Give up! You're going to die out here! This is stupid! Go back to that warm cosy cabin where hot tea is waiting. You can tell everyone back home that there was a storm, no one needs to know you quit. Come on, it's not worth it. Just turn around and go back to the warm."

Many times I came so close to giving up. I dropped to my knees, moaned that I couldn't go on, that it was too hard. Every time the team and the guides talked me around. "Come on mate, just a few more steps. You're doing so well. Let's just get to that rock up there then we'll take a little break. You've got this!"

Finally after hours of this gruelling torture, by some miracle we made it to the summit of Mt Toubkal. And my God, that moment was euphoric! We all just collapsed into a little heap at the top, hugged and high-fived, then sat in silence taking in the magnificent views. From the peak, there are unrestricted views in every direction, from the Marrakesh Plain to the High Atlas in the north and as far south as the Anti-Atlas and the Sahara. The wind dropped, the sun came out, and we laid there basking in its warmth feeling overwhelmingly happy and proud of our achievement.

I learned that day what you can truly push yourself to do when you try hard enough, and just how much more you have in the tank than you'll ever know. I often credit that single experience with changing my life, and giving me a mental strength I didn't know I had. When we're out on a walk and get caught in a heavy downpour, I laugh and think "this is nothing compared to icy snow blasting me in the face!" When I need to get a proposal out but I'm tired, I say to myself "you're tired? This isn't even close to what true tiredness is!" When I've upset someone and I know I should apologise but don't really want to, I say "just get it over with – the 5 minutes of awkwardness you'll feel sucking up are nothing compared to those hours of horrific climbing you did to get to the top of Toubkal!"

In Business

Being a business owner quite often involves leaving our comfort zone and doing things we don't like. Firing a member of staff, pitching to a room full of suspicious directors, cold calling, phoning back a prospect who didn't hire you to ask why, dealing with angry clients, responding to threats; these are all things I've had to do quite regularly as a business owner, and are all things that are well outside of my natural introverted comfort zone.

Business is tough, and if we stay in our small little comfort zones where we're safe from threats and danger and confrontation, we'll never have what it takes to thrive as a successful business owner. There's an old saying that says "your comfort zone is a beautiful place, but nothing ever grows there." As we get older, our comfort zones shrink, and the more they shrink, the harder they are to break out of.

I regularly remind myself of some of the tough challenges I've faced in the mountains, both mentally and physically, and this helps me find the strength I need to take difficult actions in business. When I feel my comfort zone closing in, I try to take actions to expand my comfort zone again and push aside my fears.

For example, I started finishing my showers each morning with a 40 second blast of cold water. Experts say this bolsters immunity, combats depression, improves circulation, increases metabolism, and reduces inflammation. I don't know if all that is true, but what I like is every single morning it forces me out of my comfort zone. The whiney little voice in my head that tries to protect me screams "NO! DON'T DO IT! WE'RE FINE WITH WARM. KEEP THE WARM ON!" and every morning I get to practice silencing this little voice and say "Thank you for the warning brain. Now shut up and get out of my way!" and on goes the cold.

I find this is a simple and relatively easy, low-discomfort way to train me to override my brain's warnings, and I'll admit it does feel quite euphoric! Once I've done this, the next time in the day I have to do something uncomfortable and the old whiney-voice kicks in, it's much easier to silence it.

For example my brain might say: *"but what if the prospect rejects you? Then you'll be upset, wouldn't it just be easier if you didn't bother calling them and just sent them an email? We could do it from the café. Yeah let's do that. Go to the café and treat yourself to a nice hot chocolate and send them a little email, don't bother making that call."* And because I've already successfully silenced old whiney-voice once that day, I say *"thank you for the warning brain, now fuck off and get out of my way!"*

Action Points

Write a list of five things that you really should be doing as a business owner, but don't like to because they're outside your comfort zone. You may be struggling to find one, or you may have hundreds. Go for five, so that we don't get overwhelmed.

Now, for each point you have written down, write ONE task to help you leave your comfort zone. Try to find a way of making it positive. For example:

Problem: I need to have a chat with an employee about their performance, but find this sort of thing very difficult.

Solution: Invite all employees in for a quarterly "1-2-1 coffee chat" where you remove the formality, have a chat about what has been going well, and also highlight areas for improvement to make next quarter even better.

Problem: you need to follow up with a prospect, but find calling people daunting.

Solution: phone some competitors from a withheld number and tell them you're starting a new company called "The Toilet Block Doc" and ask for information on their services. Try to keep them on the phone as long as possible, going into as much graphic detail as possible about some of the blocked toilets you've had to deal with. I want you to turn the idea of cold calling into an entertaining, non-frightening experience. Plus you never know, you might just sniff out some enlightening competitors' information!

Problem: you need to call back a customer who is angry about something and wants to have a good moan, but you hate this sort of confrontation.

Solution: do your best exaggerated impression of your client having a good whine about how terrible you are to your team and get them all laughing. Then say "right here we go, let's see how close I was to the mark!" and go make the call. Chances are it won't be half as bad as your exaggerated impression was!

Mt Toubkal Summit, Morocco

Leading the team through the fog in the Swiss Alps

12

Practice Gratitude

One of the things I enjoy most about mountaineering is getting to experience and learn more about other cultures and people around the world. You learn so much about different ways of life, different perspectives, and of course different ways of cooking!

I think the people that impressed me the most and really stand out in my mind when I think back to all the places I have been are the Nepalese who live and work up in the Himalayas. For two weeks we lived among them during our Everest Base Camp Trek. I won't sugar coat it... their way of living is HARD. It is so far from our typical Western comfort zones that by the end of the two weeks I was very happy to get back down from the mountains. Let me describe the small glimpse we had into their lives...

Up in the Himalayas, there are entire towns and even cities that are completely cut off from all civilisation. No roads, airports, grid connectivity etc. The only way in or out is by foot. The nearest well supplied "town" is Lukla which is a three day mountain trek away, and Lukla really is tiny! From Lukla it's a short flight by plane into

PRACTICE GRATITUDE

Kathmandu if you want to get to a "proper" city. The buildings have no electricity; some of the hotels have solar panels now but mountain weather makes these unreliable, and often the lights would go out by about 7pm. To boil a kettle, they place a metal pot in the middle of an array of mirrors which directs the sun's heat onto the pot. Unbelievably this does actually work, but takes approximately three hours to boil. Imagine having to wait three hours for a cup of tea!

There's no WIFI (*some hotels did have WIFI but I never actually found anywhere where it worked,*) there's no heating; only the main communal dining room would have a fire place. We were there in summer, and it still gets down to -10°C at night, and there's no double glazing either. So that means sleeping in your coat, hat, warm sleeping bag and several blankets. How there are any babies made in the Himalayas is a mystery!

There is no running water, it has to be collected from a near-by stream. Toilets are flushed by pouring a bucket down them. I think I managed to only get one hot shower for the whole time I was up there. There are very limited shops selling very limited supplies, and a lot of what you find in there will be well past its use-by date. The food is very limited; there's no meat up there because the people are Buddhist and won't slaughter animals (*you can see meat or dairy on the menus sometimes which has been imported from Kathmandu, but we were very strongly advised to avoid it at all costs if we didn't want to get sick! One girl in our group got a Hot Chocolate forgetting about the dairy rule and spent the whole next day throwing up.*) For two weeks we pretty much had the same choice of limited meal options: Dhal, vegetable chow mein, chips, rice. Some days I'd be starving but just couldn't stomach eating the same bland food again so went without a meal.

The people are hard workers; we'd see the women up at 5am digging up potatoes from their gardens and prepping meals for the day. Often the men would be away for weeks at a time working as sherpas, taking tourists up into the mountains.

So yes, after two weeks of living like this, I'll be honest – I was quite tired of it and ready to go back to my nice comfortable heated modern house with hot showers and proper food back in the UK! However, I was constantly reminded how the Nepalese people live like this every single day for their whole lives! There is no comfy warm house to go back to, no lovely hot shower at the end of the climb, no meal alternative when they get back home – this is how they have to live all of the time, and we hadn't even seen how harsh the conditions get in winter! I was particularly reminded of this when we passed an old lady climbing up the mountain carrying approximately 60kg on her back, which is my entire body weight to put things in perspective. I remember feeling ashamed about how I'd moaned the other day that my back was aching and I couldn't wait to not have to lug my backpack around any more.

And yet, despite this very hard way of living, I found the people I met up in the Himalayas the warmest, happiest, most welcoming people I have ever come across. They'd always greet you with a big warm smile, always stop and chat, were always patient, and they never seemed put out or annoyed.

I believe this is partly because when you don't have much, you are grateful for that which you do have. When your expectations are set so low, anything that exceeds your expectations makes you happy. For example, if all you are expecting is bread and jam for breakfast, and then one morning you find that the hotel you're in has served scrambled eggs, you're so happy to not have bread and jam! In the West we have a culture of always expecting everything to be perfect, meaning we are constantly let down and disappointed when expectations aren't met, which leads to unhappiness.

The Himalayan people are not entitled and do not expect any handouts. They have to work very hard for every single thing that they have, therefore they take nothing for granted and appreciate everything.

The whole "rat race" capitalist model for success does not exist up there. Nobody has a car, there are no designer brands, no latest iPhone, no Rolexes, no Instagram lifestyle. Everybody is just living as their true self without trying to create a false façade to impress others.

I can honestly say that the time in the Himalayas changed my life, and gave me a new perspective of things. It taught me to be very grateful for everything that I have, to want for nothing, to appreciate everything, and to understand just how incredibly rich you are if you can flick a switch and boil a kettle, have electricity, eat whatever you want, and drink the water out of the tap.

In Business

Running a business is tough. Very tough. Often it feels like a never-ending mountain climb, with ups and downs and highs and lows and good times and bad times. It's very easy to feel fed up with your business and want to pack it all in, particularly after a challenging couple of weeks! Trust me, I've been there – many, many times.

Practicing gratitude is a really good way to help you get through these tough times, and helps put things in perspective. Whenever I'm having a "I want to pack it all in" week, I write a gratitude list, of all the things I am grateful for that running a business allows me to do. For example:

- I get to choose my own hours
- I don't need anyone's permission to take time off
- Business pays for our house and puts food on our plate
- I can delegate or outsource anything that I don't enjoy doing
- No one else can put a ceiling on how much I earn
- The private medical insurance and 24/7 virtual GP appointments I get through my business
- The new MacBook Pro and annual phone upgrade that my business pays for
- I have a fantastic network of contacts and clients in all sorts of industries, who have been on hand to help me out with all sorts of issues outside of business *(everything from landscape gardening to printing stationery for our wedding!)*

Action Points

Write your own Gratitude List, of all the good things running your business gives you and that you are grateful for.

Every time you get that feeling that you are becoming fed up with running the business and are considering throwing in the towel, take a few minutes to re-visit your Gratitude List and remind yourself of all the lovely benefits you have from being a business owner, and all that you stand to lose should you go back to being a full-time employee.

PRACTICE GRATITUDE

Basic villages high up in the Himalayas, Nepal. No electricity, water, Wifi, roads or gas.

13

Find your why

It was 3am, Hoàng Liên Son Mountains of north-western Vietnam, and for several hours I'd restlessly laid awake on my flimsy excuse of a mattress that had been lazily tossed on the floor, watching rats running around the rafters above where we lay with my head pounding from too much "happy water." *(We never did find out what happy water was; some suggested it was rice wine, whilst a Google search states "Happy Water is made by dissolving other drugs – typically ecstasy, methamphetamine, diazepam, caffeine, and tramadol" – so I guess we'll never really know!)* As I watched the rats chase each other and listened to the sound of the torrential rain relentlessly pounding on the roof, I decided I could ignore my grumbling stomach no more, and that I must make the soggy dash across the forecourt to the outside toilet block.

Dressed in just my pants, raincoat and hiking boots (*an absolutely ridiculous spectacle I'm sure!*), I opened the front door, stepped out into the pitch-black night, and started to cross the forecourt. Suddenly, I heard a torrent of angry barking and snarling and galloping paws coming up behind me from an infuriated dog, running at me fast! I ran like I had never run before, and slammed that toilet door shut behind me just at the same moment the dog-monster caught up and slammed itself full-force into the toilet door.

As I stood there, shamefully emptying my bowels over the disgusting squat-drop toilet, watching the two rusty little screws holding the lock in place wriggle dangerously in their sockets and doing their very best to withstand the angry dog scrabbling at the door, whilst trying my best not to throw up from the horrific stench of soiled toilet roll piled up in the corner (*apparently flushing isn't a thing up there!*) I think it's fair to say I hit my rock-bottom, my *"Why the hell am I here"* moment.

After 15 minutes when things had finally gone quiet, I cautiously unlocked the door and peeped out. Instantly a chorus of barking and running erupted; apparently a few of the dogs' mates had come over to see what the excitement was about and join in the hunt. I slammed the door back shut, and stayed hidden in that disgusting toilet for over an hour until first light came and I was able to safely see that the dogs had gone.

When I finally crawled into bed at nearly 5 in the morning, my then-girlfriend-now-wife sleepily said "where the hell have you been all night?"

"Hiding in the toilet. I got chased by a dog."

"Oh yeah I did hear that" she said, before rolling over and promptly falling back asleep.

Anyway, the point I'm making with this entertaining but sorry story is that I think it's fair to say that most people at some point will experience a low point like this on a tough multi-day trek. It's different for each person and each trip; it could be when the altitude sickness gets you and you feel like you can't go on anymore, or when a freezing icy gale is blasting you in the face, or when you're in your tent shivering yourself to sleep wishing you were curled up in your warm cosy bed back home.

Inevitably you will ask yourself "Why. Why am I here? Why do I do these things? Why didn't I just stay at home and watch Netflix and drink beer and be happy?" Without a strong answer, these dark moments can defeat you. They can spoil the trip, cause you to give up and quit, prevent you from having adventures like this again.

I always find a strong "why" is essential to get you through these moments. It won't stop them from occurring, but it will ensure you don't stay in that place for too long, and will help you get back in the zone as quickly as possible.

Everybody's "why" is different. For some it could be a charity fundraiser to raise critical funds for an important cause. For others it could be to prove a point, either to themselves or friends or a partner. Some just like to push themselves to the limit in order to grow and develop.

For me personally, it's because I want to be on my death bed one day knowing that I lived life to the full, had the best adventures, and experienced everything life had to offer. A wise lady I met in Peru once said to me "no one ever lays on their death bed wishing they'd worked harder, or stayed later at the office. They lay there wishing they'd done more, lived more, lived life to the full." My greatest fear is not living life to it's true extent, held back by my comfort zone and that whiney little voice in my head that's trying to keep me safe by encouraging me to stay at home. When I am in these dark rock-bottom moments and my discomfort metre is at its maximum, without a strong "why" I could easily quit and slink back into my comfort zone, and never have these wonderful adventures again that ultimately end up giving me amazing stories and the most fantastic adventures of my life.

In Business

Running a business is one of the hardest things you can do; everything is always against you. It's no wonder that 70% of businesses fail within their first five years! I really believe that unless business owners have a really strong "why" as to why they started a business in the first place, it's too easy to give up and go back to your comfy day job when the going gets tough.

I believe one of the key differences between business owners who are wildly successful and business owners who fail is that the ones who are successful simply didn't quit when things got tough, they just kept going.

You think bad times don't happen to all business owners? Sure they do! I'd bet my right arm that Elon Musk felt like quitting in 2008 when SpaceX had failed it's third launch, his marriage fell apart and he was going through divorce, bankruptcy was knocking at his door, and Tesla nearly collapsed. Today Tesla is the world's most valuable automobile maker, and Elon Musk is the world's richest man, valued at $238 Billion. Imagine if he quit in 2008 when things were tough!

I've learned that the shit hits the fan for everybody; it's how you deal with it that defines whether it beats you or not.

Without a strong why, it's too easy to give up and slink back into your comfort zone when the going gets tough. It's critical you find a strong why to get you through these times and back onto your feet.

Action Points

Finding your "why" in business can be a deeply personal journey, but it's an essential one. A strong "why" not only provides motivation during challenging times but also guides decision-making and shapes your company's culture. Here are some steps to help you discover your "why":

- Self-Reflection: Spend time alone, without distractions, pondering why you started your business in the first place. What motivated you? Was it a personal experience, a gap in the market, a desire to create change, or something else?

- Look Beyond Money: Financial gain is a common reason people start businesses, but it's seldom the most compelling "why." Your "why" should be something that still matters to you even if money weren't an issue.

- Identify Your Passions: What are you truly passionate about? Your "why" is often connected to what you're passionate about – be it solving a specific problem, serving a particular community, or pursuing an interest.

- Think About Your Legacy: What mark do you want to leave on the world? How do you want your business to be remembered? This can help you identify a deeper purpose.

- Speak with Others: Talk to your co-founders, employees, or close confidants. They might see something in you or your business that you've overlooked. Their perspectives can be enlightening.

- Mission, Vision, Values: Consider your company's mission, vision, and values. Your "why" might be embedded in these. If you haven't already defined these, now is a good time to start.

- Consider Your Challenges: Sometimes, understanding why you're facing resistance or challenges can help you identify your deeper purpose. Is there something about the market, industry, or world that you're trying to change?

- Revisit Past Experiences: Think about your past, both personal and professional. There might be clues hidden in your experiences that point to your "why." For instance, a childhood experience might be driving your passion to create a particular product or service.

- Look at Your Audience: Who are your customers, and why do they choose your product or service? Sometimes, understanding your audience can help you discover or refine your "why."

Write it Down: Once you feel you've discovered your "why", write it down. This makes it tangible. Then, reflect on it regularly and check if your actions and decisions align with it. Share your "why" with trusted colleagues or mentors. Does it resonate? Does it feel authentic? Their feedback can help you refine it.

It's okay for your "why" to evolve as your business grows and as you personally change. Regularly check in with yourself and assess whether your current "why" still holds true.

Remember, your "why" is not just a marketing tool or a motivational phrase. It's the core reason your business exists and the driving force behind every decision you make. Once you've identified it, keep it front and centre. Share it with your team, embed it in your company culture, and let it guide your business towards success.

The home-stay we did in Sapa. On the right are the toilets I got trapped in

14

The importance of showing up

I'm going to let you in on a little secret. I'm not really very good at being a mountaineer. For starters, I'm terrible with heights. It's more of a fear of falling rather than actually being up high, but there have been many times on many mountain routes where internally I have been a trembling bundle of nerves. I also struggle massively with my knee. I tore the Anterior Cruciate Ligament in my left knee when I was a child, along with 85% of the cartilage, and it's troubled me ever since. It makes coming down hill painful and difficult. At 5ft6 my little legs have to work harder than my taller peers to cover the same distances in the same amount of time. And I struggle terribly with insomnia, so getting a good night's sleep on a multi-day expedition is very difficult, and leaves me fatigued and tired for the whole time. So yes, all in all, I am ashamed to say that I am not really very good at being a mountaineer at all!

So why is it that I have successfully climbed more mountains than everyone I know?

The answer is simple.... I show up. I drive to the start of a mountain, put on my boots, and start walking. Simply showing up consistently is 80% of the battle. I am not always successful in my mission; I have probably quit or failed to summit more peaks than most have even attempted. But, if I climb 100 mountains and fail at 20 of them, and the average person only climbed 20 mountains in their life, I will still have successfully summitted four times the amount of mountains than the average person, making me a wildly successful mountaineer based on nothing more than numbers and consistentcy, and absolutely nothing to do with skill.

The same is true for the martial art I train, Krav Maga. I have trained for about 12 years, and I can tell you now that I have zero natural ability. I am a slow learner when it comes to sports, and it takes me a very long time to pick things up that others pick up instantly. However, week in week out, I show up, and I train, and bit by bit I improve. I now find that often I am one of the most experienced people in the room. I still get my ass kicked by my instructor on a weekly basis and struggle learning new things, but often I am able to point out mistakes others in the class are making and help them improve, purely based on my cumulative years of experience and showing up again and again.

In Business

The same is so true in business; I honestly believe that showing up day after day after day is the key to success. Whether I'm having a great day or a terrible day, things are busy or things are quiet, I show up. And I put my head down and I get on with it. I don't believe I am particularly skilled in business, or have any natural entrepreneurial abilities. I just showed up time after time and got on with it, where others quit. In the 8 years I have been running my digital marketing agency, I have seen many fantastic agencies in our area close their doors and go under. Did we have anything special or different from them? No. We just refused to quit and kept going. Time after time.

I would say this mentality is true across many areas of business. Why is it we've got more awards than any other agency in our area? We keep entering them! Year after year, we enter. Do we win every award we enter? No. Do we keep entering regardless of our successes or losses? Yes. Are we statistically putting ourselves in a stronger position to win by consistently entering? Absolutely!

Why do we have more five star reviews than any other web design company in the UK? Is it because we're offering some amazing service that they're not? Possibly. Is it more likely because we consistently ask every client to leave us a review on Google, and remind them a couple of times if they forget? Almost definitely.

How is it that we have 100% success rate in getting our clients onto the first page of Google? Is it because we have some magic trick up our sleeve that other agencies don't know about? No. Is it because we work on their SEO every single day, and never stop looking for improvements? Of course it is!

Every single day, in my head I lace up my metaphorical mountain boots, and say "let's do this!" I don't know if I'll succeed or fail at the tasks that I set out to do that day, but the important part is I do set out to do them, again and again and again.

Action Points

1. Before you leave the office each day, write a list of every thing that you must get done tomorrow.

2. Now highlight your three most critical tasks, which are essential for business success.

3. Do those three things FIRST when you start work the next day, before you do anything else. I like to do this from home before my employees start firing questions and problems at me, and I don't open my emails or check my phone until these three things are done.

4. Find an accountability partner, someone who is also on a mission for self development in one form or another. Text them in the morning your critical business development tasks, and tell them again when they're done. Brief them to give you hell if you don't even start these tasks because "something came up."

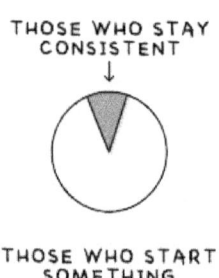

THOSE WHO STAY CONSISTENT

THOSE WHO START SOMETHING

15

Learn when to walk away

In 2022, I set out to complete one of the most challenging climbs of my life: Mt Blanc. At 4,809m, it wasn't the tallest peak I'd ever climbed, but it was set to be one of the most difficult. It had been on my bucket list for years, I'd spent 18 months getting in great shape for it, and spent a fortune on the expedition, equipment, and going away for training climbs in the Welsh mountains.

However, from the minute we got out into the high Alps, things didn't feel right. It had been an exceptionally hot summer, record-breaking in-fact, and for much of the summer it looked unlikely we would even be able to go (*French authorities actually closed the routes for a while!*) To put things into perspective, the average summit temperature on Mt Blanc should be about 0°C in summer, and this year it was averaging +10°C. Everything felt unstable; there were huge glaciers everywhere, constant rockfalls day and night where bits of the cliff faces were collapsing, and the snow was slushy and difficult to walk in.

Added to this, our guide was snappy, rude and disorganised, and lacked the calm patience you need in a good mountain guide (*he confessed that he'd planned on being retired by now, but was going through a divorce and was simply doing this for the money.*)

Overall I just had this real feeling of unease and anxiety that I couldn't shake.

Despite this, we did have a great few days up in the alps on practice walks and acclimatisation, before starting our ascent on day four. Our destination that day was the Tête Rousse Hut, which sat at an altitude of 3,167m. All went well, the trek up was wonderful, I'd been sleeping ok, and overall felt my level of fitness was great.

However, that evening, the weather started to change for the worse. A big storm hit along with heavy rain, and heavy rain usually leads to unstable mountains. The guides sat and debated amongst themselves for a long time whether or not we would attempt the summit tomorrow. Eventually they concluded that yes, we would go, but there was only a 50/50 chance the weather would permit a summit attempt. Tomorrow's trek would involve crossing the Grand Couloir (*affectionally nicknamed the Death Couloir by climbers*); a perilous crossing point which spits rocks day and night at passers by, and has claimed the lives of over 100 climbers in the last decade.

For me it was all too much. The unstable conditions, the storm which had loosened all the rocks, the guide I didn't feel safe with, the impending storm which was still to come, and of course the dangerous crossing of the Death Couloir – all for the sake of attempting a summit with only 50/50 odds of making it. For the first time in my life I did not even attempt this climb. Nothing felt right, and I made the gut-wrenching call to walk away from this one. Having spent thousands of pounds and months of my life getting in shape for this climb, it felt heart-breaking to walk away. But my gut told me it was the right decision.

The next morning I packed my bag and headed back down the mountain to the safety of Chamonix, whilst the rest of my group headed on up the mountain. From what they later told me, here's the story that followed...

- The team safely made it to the second hut (the Goûter Hut), however the weather was too bad to continue from there, meaning they'd risked crossing the deadly Grand Couloir for nothing.

- Two guys who were climbing without a guide decided to attempt the climb anyway. One of the guys was literally blown off the edge of the mountain; his climbing partner dived in the other direction and saved his life (they were roped together), however in doing so sliced his leg badly on his crampons. They were able to limp back to the Goûter Hut, however no helicopter was able to get up there due to the weather, and the conditions were too perilous to climb back down.

- Everyone was stuck up at the Goûter Hut for two days, before eventually a small window in the weather allowed for a helicopter to extract the injured climber, and my group were able to make it back down the mountain. However, they said this involved scrabbling down over slippery rocks covered in snow and ice from the storm, and they were rushing because the weather window was so short.

When we caught up after the expedition back in England, they all said they wished they'd headed back down with me, and described it as one of the most horrific experiences of their lives.

In Business

Sometimes in business, I have found that just like on Mont Blanc, one must know when to walk away from a bad deal. This can be difficult when the deal is worth a lot of money, especially when times are quiet and cashflow is limited. But I have learned the hard way that sometimes a difficult client can cost you far more in time and energy than they are worth in financial reward, particularly if they end up taking so much of your time that you could have serviced ten clients in the same time it took you to look after this one.

I had a perfect example of this happen recently; a client had just signed up for a 12 month contract worth £10k+ per month. I should have been elated by such a deal, however something felt wrong about it. The client was just a little bit too keen, too willing to move forward, and seemed to have too much money for a company which didn't even have a website yet. Again I had a feeling of unease I couldn't shake, and was struggling to sleep. I decided we would tentatively go ahead with the contract, but at the first sign of trouble we would pull the plug.

Well by the end of that first week and before the client had sent over a single penny, he had already started trying to drastically move the goal posts – insisting things which should have taken 6 weeks to complete were finished within 3 days, and insisting that we had agreed to include extra things free of charge beyond our original scope. Despite the impressive size of the contract, I concluded that if the client was like this so early into the project, how would he behave after he'd actually paid us? I made the executive decision to walk away, and politely told the client that I was very sorry but I felt we weren't a good fit for his business and he should find an agency more suited to his needs. The client did not take this well, and posted long angry ranting reviews across our social networks.

If things were that bad so early on before he'd actually paid us, they certainly would not have been great a few months down the line when significant amounts of money had been paid.

Just like on Mont Blanc, I have no doubt that walking away was the right decision. Sometimes the promise of the reward is just not worth the cost.

Action Points

1. Think of a time when you had a bad client or a bad project that was way more hassle than it was worth, or things went badly.

2. Think back very carefully to your first meetings. Where there any warning signs, uneasy feelings, or something that wasn't right? See if you can pinpoint anything that was out of place.

3. Write down all the signs, and add them to a list of "things to walk away from."

4. Now make a list of any clients who are causing you headaches and taking up too much of your time. Fire them. They're not worth it.

I have done this exercise for every client relationship that hasn't worked out well, and every time when I look back, there were very obvious signs there right at the start that this was going to be a bad deal and this client would come with problems. I wish I'd had the wisdom and confidence back then that I have now to walk away from deals like this.

They say 80% of your problems come from 20% of your clients; I have found this to be very true. Being a business owner is tough enough without bad clients adding to your problems. Learn to trust your gut, walk away from bad deals, and drop D-grade clients.

Stormy weather on Mt Blanc, France

16

Pain Vs Discomfort

There have been many times in the mountains, probably every climb in fact, where at some point or another I've wanted to turn back and go home. Climbing often pushes us to the limit, and whether it's the altitude making you nauseous, fatigue making you mentally exhausted, or bad weather literally dampening your spirits, mountain climbing is as much a mind game as it is physical challenge.

During these moments, your brain's primary warning system, the system that was put in place to say "*Shit - saber tooth tiger! Run run run!*" starts to get really uncomfortable. Whilst logically we understand we're in safe hands with an experienced guide, food and shelter is waiting for us an hour away, and we're roped up to minimise danger, your primary alarm system is thinking "*hostile terrain, exposed cliffs, no food, no shelter. Ohh this is not good. This is not good at all! Better sound the alarm and turn back to safety before we die of hypothermia or starvation up here!*"

This internal warning system is designed to keep us safe, but it's crucial to distinguish between genuine danger or pain and mere discomfort when climbing. Millennia of evolution has fine-tuned our brains to be a top-notch security system. And while that's impressive, it's not always helpful in our modern context.

There's been many times where I've been hanging onto a cliff side or climbing wall, feeling the pull of gravity and the strain in my muscles, and that primal part of my brain doesn't understand the thrill of the climb, nor the safety of the rope and harness. Instead, it sees potential death. My fear of heights means I've struggled with this a lot; even though I know I am roped up and safe, there have been a lot of times where I've been frozen in fear and trembling like a leaf despite not actually being in any danger.

In these moments when you're an hour away from the summit, the wind is blasting you in the face, you're physically exhausted and your brain is screaming at you to go back down to safety and comfort, it's vital to pause and assess. Are you truly in pain or in real danger? Have you pulled a muscle, twisted an ankle, or cut yourself? Or are you just uncomfortable with the situation? Are you just tired, out of breath, or feeling the pressure against your palms?

Genuine pain is your body's SOS – a clear signal that something is wrong. Discomfort, on the other hand, is often a temporary sensation, resulting from pushing your boundaries or adapting to a new situation, and leaving your comfort zone.

I like to personify that cautionary voice in my head. We'll call him "Brian." Brian means well. He's the reason our ancestors survived. But in today's world, especially on a mountain climb, Brian can be a royal pain in the arse!

So, the next time I'm grappling with a particularly challenging stretch and Brian screams, "*Retreat to safety! You can't do this!*" I kindly respond, "*Thank you for the warning, Brian. Now shut up and let me climb.*"

Remember, these internal alerts from your brain are just that – warnings. You don't have to act on them. By recognising the difference between actual pain or danger and temporary discomfort, you can make informed decisions. Always ensure your safety, but don't let Brian's over protective warnings prevent you from experiencing the exhilaration of the climb. The next time discomfort comes knocking, thank Brian for his concern, assess the situation, and continue your ascent with confidence and clarity.

In Business

Often in business we have to do things that make us very uncomfortable. Like mountaineering, I believe being a business owner is as much about mental strength and resilience as it is about skill and intelligence. It's very easy to feel doubt and panic when shit hits the fan in business, and I find it's a constant journey of separating genuine concern from mere discomfort and pushing past the voices of doubt.

Whether you're launching a new product, running a new promotion, or trialing a new marketing campaign, running a business is continuously stepping into unknown territory. The potential risks and uncertainties can be overwhelming. That's when our old friend "Brian," that ever-cautious caveman voice echoing with warnings of potential death and highlighting the comforts of a stable, predictable job wakes up. Brian will remind you of every potential downside, every challenge, and every uncertainty.

"*Don't call that lead back, they might reject us! Rejection could mean *expulsion from the village, starvation and death!"* your brain is thinking, *"and don't even think about having that awkward chat with that employee who isn't performing, they might react badly and attack us and we could get killed! Even more death! And don't you dare hire that marketing agency, if it fails and we lose money we might not be able to buy food and then we'll certainly starve to death!"* These are the sort of subconscious thought patterns that your brain's protection system is thinking of constantly which override rational thought, and the kind of negative self talk that will keep you in your comfort zone and stop you from hitting your potential.

As with mountain climbing, it's imperative you learn to differentiate between genuine business pain or danger and temporary discomfort. Like with the body, genuine pain is an indication that something in your business isn't working and requires immediate attention. Maybe a marketing strategy isn't yielding results, a product has glaring defects, or there's a significant cash flow issue.

Discomfort on the other hand is the inevitable unease that comes with growth and venturing into the unknown. Maybe you're launching a new product, expanding into a new market, or hiring for roles you've never managed before. The unease is a natural reaction to change but not necessarily a sign that things are going awry.

Every time you're about to take a business risk or embark on a new venture, and Brian shouts, *"This is too risky! Maybe it's not worth it. Stay where you are, avoid death"* remember to acknowledge the warning but also put it into perspective. *"Thank you, Brian, for your caution. I've assessed the risks, and I'm prepared to move forward."*

Armed with data, research, and preparation, as businesses owners we must learn to trust our judgment. While it's essential to consider Brian's warnings, being paralyzed by them can be detrimental. Recognise the warnings as just that—cautionary notes. They serve as reminders to double-check our strategies, revisit our plans, or sometimes pivot entirely. Yet, they shouldn't deter us from the path of innovation and growth.

Embracing discomfort is often a sign of stepping out of your comfort zone, innovating, and breaking new ground. If I'm comfortable then I'm not growing, and in business if I'm not growing then I'm shrinking.

Every business owner will face their fair share of hypothetical mountains to climb. By understanding the nature of challenges, both internal and external, you can navigate the business landscape with clarity, resilience, and determination. The next time you face business discomforts, acknowledge your inner Brian, reassess your strategies, and march ahead with unwavering focus.

Action Points

1. Mindfulness and Meditation: Begin with a daily practice of mindfulness or meditation. It can help you centre your thoughts, gain clarity, and develop the skill to observe warnings without reacting impulsively. For me this is my morning dog walk; a chance to quietly reflect without interruption. Over time, you'll be better equipped to respond to challenges with calmness and deliberate action, rather than being overwhelmed by immediate emotions.

2. Journaling: I find writing a daily or weekly journal to jot down my fears, doubts, and concerns really helps prevent them from spiraling around my head.

3. Continuous Learning: Equip yourself with knowledge. By staying updated in your industry and continuously learning, you'll build confidence in your decisions. Read books, and attend workshops, webinars, and conferences. The more informed you are, the quieter "Brian" becomes.

4. Mentorship and Networking: Connect with mentors or peers in your industry. Sharing your concerns with someone experienced can offer valuable insights and perspective. They might have faced similar challenges and can guide you with tried-and-tested solutions or approaches.

5. Risks & Contingency: Conduct regular risk assessments for your business. By identifying potential pitfalls in advance and planning for them, you'll feel more in control. Having contingency plans eases the anxiety of the unknown.

6. Celebrate Small Wins: Every milestone, no matter how small, is a testament to your progress. Celebrate them. Recognising and rewarding progress can counterbalance the voices of doubt and provide motivation for the journey ahead.

7. Limit Exposure to Negativity: While it's essential to be aware of potential challenges, continuously focusing on negative news or pessimistic projections can amplify inner doubts. The news will have you believe that society is permanently on the brink of collapse! Consume information mindfully and maintain a balance between staying informed and remaining optimistic. Personally I avoid the news - it's always negative!

8. Engage in Physical Activity: I have always found that physical exercise, whether it's a daily walk, yoga, martial arts or gym workouts, or of course a mountain climb, help in managing stress and clearing your mind by purging physical stress from the body. A clear mind is more adept at distinguishing between genuine concerns and unfounded fears.

A photo of me looking out across the Himalayas at approx 4,000m. Worth the discomfort of a little altitude sickness!

17

Climbing is better with friends

Don't get me wrong, I do enjoy a good solo climb now and again. It's a rare opportunity for peace and quiet, and gives me a nice opportunity to gather my thoughts and formulate ideas without interruption. However, there's no doubting that some of my favourite memories have been made climbing with friends!

I remember the stories shared on the long walks, the laughs and pranks we'd play on each other, teasing each other's struggles to lighten the mood, and being there for one another to egg each other on and get them through the challenging points.

Like the time in Switzerland where we'd all had a few beers and I was laughing so hard that I couldn't catch my breath in the thin air and almost passed out. Or the Three Peaks Challenge I did with a bunch of mates that felt like a school trip without any teachers present to tell us off. Or the long ascent up Dead Woman's Pass in Peru where I couldn't walk more than a few metres before needing to stop and catch my breath, and a kind lady walked and chatted with me the entire way to ensure I wasn't alone and didn't give up (*interestingly I never saw her again at the camp or for the rest of the trek. To this day I don't know if she was real or a hallucination caused by hypoxia and exhaustion!)*

Mountain terrains are unpredictable. There are moments when the path gets rough, the weather turns treacherous, or fatigue sets in. In such moments, the collective energy of a group acts as a fantastic pillar of support. When one person feels disheartened, the others rally around, offering words of encouragement and sharing their own experiences. This shared motivation ensures that everyone keeps moving, no matter how challenging the climb.

Being a part of a group often brings out the best in us. There's an innate desire to match the group's pace, energy, and enthusiasm. If everyone else is pushing forward with vigour, you're naturally inclined to summon your strength and keep up. It's not just about fitting in; it's about harnessing the collective spirit to overcome individual limitations.

And nothing beats that incredible feeling of all reaching the summit together after a difficult climb. There's something profoundly fulfilling about celebrating with those who understand the journey and the hardships faced, and the immense effort it took to reach that point. Often I've found lifelong friends during such treks. These relationships, built on trust and shared experiences, add an emotional richness to the journey.

In Business

Running a business is tough. Really tough. And lonely. You often have to make difficult decisions, do unpleasant things, and shoulder an awful lot of responsibility. I remember the conversation I had with my coach once when I was considering bringing a business partner on board:

"What's the real reason you want to bring him on as a business partner Joe?"

"He has a lot of skills that I don't, I think he'd bring a lot to the table."

"Bullshit. Joe give me the real reason."

"I dunno, I guess I'm just a bit lonely running a business on my own."

"Joe, you want to give away 50% of your business, 50% of everything you've worked so hard to build, because you're a bit lonely? Everyone's lonely in business Joe, it's just how it is. Don't do anything stupid!"

And he was right. I almost made a terrible mistake, because I didn't want to be alone in business anymore. But I overcame it, and found ways to combat that feeling of isolation.

Having a business coach or mentor is obviously a great way to share the journey without having to give away half your business. You can tell them your struggles, concerns, losses, and wins. They'll celebrate with you when you're up and get you back on your feet when you're down.

I find having friends who are business owners can be really helpful. They "get it" in a way that people who are employed just don't. Be careful with this though, being friends with business owners who are negative or small minded can really hold you back and stunt your growth, ideally you want to be friends with people who run businesses bigger than yours, so they drag you up to their level.

Building a solid team really helps too. If you hire people who you genuinely trust that have more experience than you, their opinions can really help guide your decisions and ease the loneliness.

Finally hiring decent consultants helps massively. Got a staff issue? Find an HR consultant. Got a financial issue? Speak to your accountant. Got a legal issue? Speak to a lawyer. Joining your local chamber of commerce gives you support with these things, and can be a good way of having a quality support network to bounce ideas off.

Ultimately, whether you're climbing a mountain or running a business, it can be a lonely experience, but it doesn't have to be. Surrounding yourself with as many good people as possible will make the journey a lot easier.

Me (third from the left) and a group of mates on the Three Peaks Challenge

18

Invest in the right tools

When I reminisce about my early climbing days, I vividly remember the enthusiasm of being a student with a heart full of passion and pockets full of air. Being a poor student with no money often meant I struggled to investment in quality equipment. Opting for budget-friendly gear was my only choice, as funds were limited. But as the saying goes, "A cheap man pays twice," and my experiences were testament to this.

During one climb in the Swiss Alps for example; mid-climb, as I leaned on my budget trekking pole for support, it suddenly snapped in half, leaving me without my vital support for my dodgy knee that always gives me problems in rugged terrain. This could have been easily avoided had I invested in quality over cost; a good trekking pole should last for life!

Or for example, although my adventures in the Andes Mountains in Peru were memorable, I struggled a lot with the biting cold. Every night, wrapped in my budget sleeping bag, I found myself shivering with cold and unable to sleep. I lost vital sleep which really put a damper on the whole trek because of a decision to save some money on gear. I don't think I slept a wink for four days straight, which meant I was like a walking Zombie by the end of the trek and struggled with energy the whole time.

Another example of my terrible life choices was found with a pair of cheap waterproof trousers I had bought. Waterproof trousers are meant to keep the rain and moisture out, but my budget trousers weren't breathable; instead of protection, they trapped moisture on the inside, leaving me damp and uncomfortable. Not only was it unpleasant, but it was also potentially dangerous given the cold conditions. The very equipment meant to protect me from the harsh conditions was making things worse.

The initial savings from cheap equipment often resulted in greater expenses, either in replacements, compromised safety, or the discomfort I endured. It became abundantly clear that in the mountains, quality equipment isn't just a luxury; it's a necessity.

Whilst budget constraints are real, especially for budding enthusiasts, it's essential to recognise the long-term value of quality gear. Sometimes, it's better to wait, save up, and invest in equipment that not only enhances the mountain climbing experience but also ensures safety and comfort. After all, in the harsh terrains of the mountains, we need all the help we can get. And as climbers, we must equip ourselves with nothing but the best.

In Business

Much like the demanding world of mountain climbing, running a business is filled with challenges and uncertainties. And in both terrains, the tools and resources we choose to rely on play a pivotal role in determining our success. The lessons learned from my cost saving tactics in the mountains translate seamlessly into the world of business.

When launching a start-up, resources are often limited. There's an overwhelming desire to bootstrap, cut costs, and seek shortcuts. Just as I once opted for budget mountain gear, many business owners are tempted to choose inexpensive solutions over quality investments. I know, I've been there! But as I learned in the mountains, cheap can come at a high price. I remember my first business laptop; it was an HP Windows machine and the guy in PC World described it *"basically the same as a MacBook Pro but half the price."* Four months later the thing was useless; it ran so slowly it was unusable and unsellable. I had to fork out for the MacBook Pro in the end... I paid half and I paid twice.

I also remember our early days of hosting where we opted for a low-cost server solution for our clients in order to save costs. But that cost saving came at a price; the whole platform crashed, leading to down-time for a lot of our clients *(including our own website)*, non-existent support, and a raft of furious emails and angry phone calls. We lost a lot of our clients that month, and I came very close to giving up and shutting down the business. Much like the snapped trekking pole in the Swiss Alps, a compromised business infrastructure can fail you when you need it the most. Eventually I found a very robust *(albeit expensive!)* hosting solution, and worked solidly for five days straight migrating all of our clients over to the new solution. Ultimately we learned our lesson and today offer a bullet-proof hosting solution for our clients, but I still shiver at the thought of how close I came to throwing in the towel that month.

Another harsh learning curve was choosing to hire employees on lower salaries, because it was all I could afford at the time! Operational inefficiencies, lack of expertise, embarrassing mistakes and poor customer

INVEST IN THE RIGHT TOOLS

service made by under qualified personnel can cost a business much more in the long run, both in terms of money and reputation. I remember spending so much time re-doing the work of my former staff because I hadn't paid people with proper experience and skill. Now I've learned if I can't afford to hire skilled people and pay them properly, don't hire them at all.

Opting for cheaper solutions might seem like saving money, but hidden costs often lurk beneath the surface. Just as my "waterproof" trousers let me down, seemingly cost-effective business solutions can lead to longer turnaround times, inferior service quality, or subpar customer experiences.

Every entrepreneur should understand that initial cost-saving measures might lead to greater expenses down the line, whether through repairs, replacements, or lost opportunities. Instead, focus on the value offered by quality investments. The tools and resources we invest in can either propel us forward or hold us back. The initial costs of quality might be higher, but the dividends they pay in terms of reliability, efficiency, and peace of mind are invaluable.

Action Points

1. Prioritise Infrastructure Investments: Periodically review the technologies and platforms your business relies on. Ensure they are robust, secure, and scalable. Investing in reliable infrastructure now can prevent costly downtime and inefficiencies in the future. As you envision your business scaling, ensure your infrastructure can handle the increased load, whether it's server capacity, physical space, or logistics management.

2. Focus on Talent Acquisition and Retention: While budget constraints are real, prioritise hiring individuals who bring not only the right skills but also align with your company's values and culture. I find continuous training and professional development opportunities amplify your team's productivity and loyalty. This not only benefits the business in terms of output but also enhances employee satisfaction and retention.

3. Be Wary of False Economies: Before choosing a vendor or solution based solely on cost, do thorough research. Look for reviews, test the product or service, and assess its long-term value. Regularly evaluate the products, services, and tools you're investing in. Ensure that what might seem like a bargain isn't costing you more in hidden fees, inefficiencies, or compromised quality.

A good trekking pole will last you for life, if you invest in a decent one!

19

If you can't change your environment, change your mindset

It was on the 8th day of our trek to Everest Base Camp that it hit me. That sinking low point where you just wished you were back home curled up on the sofa under a nice warm blanket. It was a long day, we'd just crossed 5,000m, and the altitude was getting to me. I was tired, fed up, the wind was howling in my ears, the sun was hiding away behind dark clouds, and my feet didn't want to do any more walking. I was lagging behind the others at the back of the group, regretting my terrible life choices and wishing I was anywhere but here.

"Why do you do this to yourself? Just tell the guide you're struggling and ask him to take you back. You don't need to do this" said Brian, the name I've given to the annoying voice in my head that tries to protect me but fills my head with constant doubt and negativity.

"*Shut up Brian, you're not helping!*" I said to myself.

Suddenly, I heard my business coach's voice in my head saying "If you can't change your mindset, change your environment." With our modern ways of living, changing our environment is something we've become very used to. If it's too cold we turn on the heating. If it's too hot we turn on the aircon. If it's raining we go inside. If it's too loud we find a different venue. We have become fully accustomed to being in almost total control of our environments all the time, so changing our mindset is not something we are well practiced in doing.

However, in the mountains, we cannot change our environment. We have to embrace the elements no matter what, and endure whatever the mountains throw at us. Often there is no shelter, no escape, and the nearest place of comfort is hours and hours away.

So how, how could I change my mindset, seeing as there was no way I could alter my environment? How could I snap out of this destructive negative mindset I'd found myself in? I racked my brain for a solution, and then I had an idea. I remembered that deep in my bag somewhere was a pair of headphones I'd chucked in at the last minute in case I got bored in the huts and wanted to listen to music. So I got out my headphones, put them on, and put on my absolute favourite motivational music (*a London Grammar set list played by Annie Nightingale if you're interested, you can find it on YouTube.*)

What happened next was incredible. First, with the sound of the howling wind cancelled out, I realised that actually I could not feel the wind through my wind-proof jacket and warm clothing, and the psychological impact of the sound of the wind howling had made it seem far worse than it actually was. Next, as my mood lifted, I started to notice just how stunning my surroundings were. I started to list all the things I was grateful for; how lucky I was to be having this fantastic adventure, how grateful I was that I had an able body which allowed me to make this trek (dodgy knee aside!), and how insightful it was to be able to experience different people and cultures around the world.

I then did a little check in with myself, asking what was the reality of the situation. "On a scale of 0-10, with 0 being no pain and 10 being absolute agony, how much pain are my feet in? Only a two?! Oh wow, we need to stop moaning about that then! What about tiredness, with 0 being you're fully energised, and 10 being as exhausted as you were that time you summitted Mt Toubkal. Only a four?! Damn Joe, you summitted Toubkal when you were 10/10 exhausted! This is NOTHING!"

I realised that actually things were no way near as bad as I'd told myself they were, and in reality I was in much better condition than I thought I was. My mood wasn't just lifted, I was purely elated!

With my favourite motivational music blaring in my ears, I heard nothing but joyful tunes, saw nothing but majestic surroundings, and felt nothing but pure euphoria. Without meaning to, I power-walked up that mountain, flew past everyone in the group, and within a few minutes was springing along joyfully next to the lead guide who looked at me with concern and asked what drugs I'd taken.

Nothing physically changed, either in my body or in the environment, but mentally the situation became wholly different when my mindset shifted and I viewed things through a different paradigm.

In Business

"What's the matter with you?" my business coach asked me one day, as I stood pacing around his office in a foul mood, angry and irritable.

"Eugh, I'm so frustrated! All of our clients are being rude and disrespectful. Everyone's just being really horrible right now."

"Joe, stop right there" said my coach, "I need you to write down a list of all of your clients that you have right now."

"Ok, done." I sighed.

"Good, and now circle all the ones who are being rude and disrespectful."

I complied.

"Good. How many clients have you got currently, and of those how many have you circled as being rude?"

"Well..." I replied reluctantly, gazing down at my list, "we're working with 12 clients currently. And of those 12, I've circled 2 that are giving us grief."

"Two?!" my coach yelled, "Two out of twelve clients are being rude, and you've come in here ranting about how ALL of your clients are being rude right now?!"

It seemed silly. I felt ashamed of myself, and embarrassed about what a brat I'd been and how consumed I'd been for such a small percentage of clients who were actually causing problems. Just like in the mountains where I was moaning about my feel being in pain for a measly 2/10, again I was not putting my problems into perspective, and was letting the things that were bad completely overshadow the things that were good. I was letting my problems consume me, and distract from the reality of just how positive things actually were.

IF YOU CAN'T CHANGE YOUR ENVIRONMENT, CHANGE YOUR MINDSET

I left my coach's office ashamed but having learned an important lesson that day; always put your problems into perspective, and always look for ways to change your mindset if you can't change your environment.

Action Points

1. Write down a list of anything that is bothering you in business. Anything at all, from rude clients, financial problems, lack of leads, or staff issues.
2. Now score each problem out of 10, with 10 meaning it could not be any worse and 0 meaning it is not a problem at all.
3. With your issues in perspective, now write a simple "yes" or "no" under a sub heading "can I do anything to control this problem?" For example, if the problem is a difficult member of staff, then obviously the answer is yes, you do have lots of things you can do to sort this problem out. If the problem is outside of your control, such as difficult economic conditions or rising energy prices, then of course the answer is No you cannot do anything to control this problem.
4. Having identified which problems you CAN control, now write a list of action points to get these issues dealt with. Whether that means firing a member of staff, changing a supplier, dropping a bad client, or increasing your prices, make sure you don't let these problems mount up, and you take action to resolve them.
5. For problems you can't control, firstly look back to the score out of ten you gave them. Are they really so bad? If they're not really that bad at all, then it may be ok to simply make your peace with these little niggles and focus on the big picture. If they are genuinely problematic, we need to change our mindset. There's nothing we can do to control the problem, and staying in a negative head space is no good for business. Here are some steps I've always found help

me in these situations:

- Acknowledge that economic conditions will be hitting all of your competitors also. If energy prices have risen for you, they have risen for them too.
- Look at the big picture – in the scheme of things, are these issues really causing you pain? Or just temporary discomfort?
- Practice gratitude – write down a list of everything that's going really well right now in your business. Sometimes this is enough to change your mindset and focus on the positives.
- Whilst you can't control the problem, write a list of everything you can control which can allow you to mitigate it. For example, if energy prices have risen, raise your prices. If the economic climate is bad, enter new markets. If it's an employees market, hire someone overseas.

It's important to accept that in life, there are always things which are outside of our control. This is true for every single business owner on the planet. The shit hits the fan for everybody; it's how you deal with it that defines you. Only when the storm hits will the true extent of the captain's skill become apparent.

Don't let your problems define you... let your solutions.

A cold, grey, blustery hike on the climb to Everest Base Camp, Nepal

Pushing against altitude sickness in the high Alps

20

Slow and steady wins the race

We were in the heart of the Himalayas, staring up at the *Thorong La Pass* (5,416m) towering above us, our hearts pounding with anticipation. My group and I had trained for months, physically and mentally preparing ourselves for the long climb ahead. The air was thin, the weather crisp, and our determination unshakable.

But here's the thing about high-altitude mountaineering: the air up there is a harsh old sod. It's thin, it's cold, and it's got no patience for the reckless.

At about 4,000m, the first signs of trouble appeared. One of our group (let's call him Dave) started to stumble and slur his words. Dave and a couple of the lads in the group had become a little competitive in their pace, and were shooting up the mountain much faster than they should have been.

The relentless pace they had set in the thin air was quietly wreaking havoc on their bodies. They were ascending too quickly, and altitude sickness was stealthily sneaking up on them. Out of nowhere Dave slumped over, threw up, started turning blue, and lay there rapidly panting and struggling for breath. After a few minutes of emergency oxygen treatment, Dave and one of the guides had to quickly descend, leaving behind his dreams of the summit in order to return to safety.

Altitude sickness is the grim reaper of the mountains. It doesn't care about your determination, your ambitions, or your bravado. It will humble you, and it will make you pay dearly for your haste. Symptoms like nausea, headaches, dizziness, and confusion can turn even the fittest, most experienced mountaineer into a helpless prisoner of the altitude if you're not careful.

As the guide descended with Dave, I couldn't help but reflect on the importance of pacing in high-altitude climbing. The mountains teach us many lessons, and one of the most important is that patience is not just a virtue; it's a lifeline. You must respect the altitude, honour the acclimatisation process, and climb slowly, listening to your body and the respecting the dangers of the mountains.

Acclimatisation walks and rest days are critical to success when it comes to high-altitude climbing. Whilst sitting around for a day in a basic hut not doing much can feel frustrating, without acclimitisation days you're far more likely to fall victim to altitude sickness. These short walks and rest days at lower elevations help your body adapt to the thin air, allowing it to produce more red blood cells and efficiently use oxygen. And those rest days are so so important! They provide your body with much-needed recovery time, allowing it to repair and replenish itself and adapt to the low oxygen.

I used to hate rest days when I was younger. I remember thinking "*come on, we're all fine, let's just get there. What are we sitting around for?*" But experience has taught me that it's better to get there in 8 days than to try and do it in 5 and not get there at all. Ultimately if you don't take the time to properly acclimatise, no matter how fit and strong you are, it's quite likely that if you haven't taken the time to adapt, the mountain will simply turn you away and you'll be forced to head back down.

In Business

Much like mountaineering, the world of business has its own treacherous paths and dizzying heights, and the things I've learned in the mountains can serve as an important lesson for business growth.

I've had the privilege of witnessing many businesses rise to incredible heights, driven by ambition, investment, or the allure of big contracts. It's like watching a rocket take off, exhilarating and awe-inspiring. However, it's equally disheartening to see these very businesses plummet back to Earth, their dreams of success dashed.

What goes wrong? I believe that businesses can grow too big too fast. Just like Dave's ill-fated attempt to rush up Thorong La, these businesses ascended too quickly, blinded by the thrill of growth and the allure of rapid success. We had a lovely client once who won a £3 million p/a contract providing services to a major national courier. They quickly scaled their business, taking on teams, vehicles, multiple offices etc, and were enjoying the thrill of business success. Devastatingly, the courier literally cancelled their contract overnight, out of the blue one Friday afternoon. Within two weeks the business collapsed.

But here's where the analogy to mountaineering rings true. Just as altitude sickness can bring a mountaineer to their knees, the rapid expansion without proper preparation can bring a business to its breaking point. Scaling too quickly can strain resources, overwhelm teams, and expose weaknesses that were hidden beneath the surface. The systems and processes that were once manageable crumble under the weight of growth, or the sudden loss of a major client can cripple the business.

Much like the importance of acclimatisation walks and rest days in mountaineering, businesses must recognise the value of pacing themselves. Acclimatisation in business involves gradually increasing capacity and capability, allowing your team and systems to adapt to the changing demands of growth. It means investing in infrastructure, training, and processes to support your expansion.

Rest days in the business world may not involve kicking back with your feet up, but they're equally essential. These are the moments when you pause, reflect, and refine. You assess what's working and what's not, and you make the necessary adjustments. Rest days can prevent burnout, ensure the alignment of your team, and help you refocus on your long-term vision. I call them clarity days; I like to book out a day once a month to just sit in a coffee shop, with nothing more than a pen and a notebook (*leave your emails at home, this is critical!*) to reflect on where we are and gather my thoughts on where to go next. I find these so helpful; booking time in my calendar to stop and think is an underrated business activity, but a critical one!

I've seen businesses that heeded these lessons thrive and stand the test of time. They may not have skyrocketed to the top overnight, but their ascent was steady, calculated, and sustainable. They built robust foundations, nurtured their teams, and adapted to the heights they aimed to reach.

So, my fellow entrepreneurs, remember this when you're charting the course for your business. Ascend slowly, acclimatise diligently, and take those essential rest days. In doing so, you'll not only reach the summit but also build a business that can withstand the fierce winds of competition and the ever-changing terrain of the marketplace. Your journey may not be the fastest, but it will be one of resilience, wisdom, and enduring success.

Action Points

1. Embrace Sustainable Growth: Just as mountaineers pace themselves during ascents, business owners should prioritise sustainable growth. Rather than rushing to expand rapidly, focus on gradual and controlled growth. Set realistic goals for expansion and ensure that your infrastructure, team, and processes can support the increased demands. It's better to reach your goals steadily and maintain them than to rush to the summit only to tumble back down.

2. Prioritise Acclimatisation and Adaptation: In the business world, acclimatisation translates to adaptability and resilience. Invest in systems and processes that can adapt to changing market conditions and business demands. Train your team to be agile and open to change. Periodically assess your strategies, and be willing to pivot when necessary. This adaptability will help your business weather the unpredictable challenges that can arise during your journey to success.

3. Schedule Regular "Clarity Days" for Reflection and Improvement: Just as rest days are essential for mountaineers to recharge and refine their strategies, business owners should schedule regular

periods for reflection and improvement. Dedicate time to assess your business's performance, identify areas for growth and improvement, and make necessary adjustments. These "clarity days" can prevent burnout, enhance efficiency, and ensure that your business remains aligned with its long-term vision.

By applying these principles of pacing, acclimatization, and reflection, business owners can build and maintain successful enterprises that not only reach the heights they aspire to but also stand strong against the challenges of the competitive business landscape.

Pausing for a break, Mt Blanc ascent

21

The Importance of Going at Your Own Pace

The mountains have always held a special place in my heart. Their majestic peaks, serene valleys, and rugged trails have been the backdrop to some of my most cherished memories and adventures. Over the years, I've had the privilege of exploring and climbing in mountain ranges around the world, each offering unique challenges and rewards. But there's one lesson I'd like to share with you that stands out - the importance of going at your own pace.

When you're in a group, it's easy to want to match the pace of the others. You're excited, eager to prove yourself, and no one wants to be the slowest! However, I've learned the hard way that pushing yourself too hard often doesn't work in your favour in the mountains.

I remember one particular hike where this lesson truly sank in. It was my first multi-day trek with a group, and I was determined to prove myself. My little legs, shorter than the lanky buggers leading at the front, pumped vigorously to keep up with the brisk pace set by my companions. I felt the burn in my muscles and the strain in my lungs, but I kept pushing.

THE IMPORTANCE OF GOING AT YOUR OWN PACE

At first, it seemed like I was doing fine. The views were breath-taking, and the adrenaline rush fueled my determination. But as the hours passed and we gained elevation, I began to struggle. My strides grew shorter, my breath grew shallower, and my energy waned. My friends, caught up in their own rhythm, soon left me behind. I was pushing myself too hard.

It was then, when I found myself hanging back on the mountain trail with some of the slower members of the group, exhausted from over exertion, that I truly began to appreciate the significance of going at your own pace. I slowed down, taking measured steps and allowing my body to find its natural rhythm.

And find it I did. With each step, I felt a renewed sense of peace and a deep connection with the mountain. I wasn't racing against anyone else anymore; I was going at my own pace and discovering my own strength, and savouring every moment of the journey. I realised that it wasn't a race or a competition, no one was judging me for being a little slower, and all I was doing by trying to keep pace with the others was ruining my own experience.

As I continued at my own pace, something miraculous happened. I began to notice the small wonders around me—the delicate wildflowers peeking from crevices in the rocks, the graceful flight of a hawk riding the thermals, and the intricate patterns left by a wandering stream. These moments of quiet observation and reflection were the treasures of the mountain that I might have missed if I had continued to rush ahead.

Eventually, I reached the summit, albeit a few minutes later than some of my friends. But the sense of relaxation and harmony was so much nicer than if I'd pushed myself too hard in order to prove myself, where I would probably have ended up slumping down in an exhausted heap at the top. I had learned that the mountains are not just about reaching the summit; they're about the journey itself, the connection with nature, and the discovery of your own limits and strengths.

In the mountains, as in life, we all have our unique strides and our individual paces. It's a lesson worth remembering, not just on the trails but in every aspect of our lives. We shouldn't measure ourselves against others' standards or rush through our experiences. Instead, we should embrace the wisdom of going at our own pace—a pace at which we can walk all day, savouring the beauty and wonder that surround us.

So, as you embark on your own mountain adventures or any other endeavours, remember the mountains' timeless lesson. Whether your legs are long or short, your journey is yours alone, and the pace is yours to set. Embrace it, savour it, and let the mountains teach you the art of finding your stride.

In Business

In the world of business, much like in the wilderness of the mountains, there is a constant ebb and flow of success, challenge, and growth. As entrepreneurs and business owners, we often find ourselves on a journey of aspiration and ambition, seeking to reach the summits of success.

In the business world, this lesson of going at your own pace holds a mirror to the dynamics of competition and comparison that often plague us. It's easy to feel inferior or even a failure when someone new to the game seems to be making remarkable strides in a much shorter time. I remember people I know who started businesses and were making 6 figures in year 1, something that took me about 4 years to achieve. Or people who ran agencies making 5 times what ours made. These stories made me feel grossly inadequate and like a failure in business. On the flip side, it's equally easy to forget that there are those who have been in business much longer than you and yet are still doing much worse, and would envy the success you've already achieved.

The truth is, just as in the mountains, everyone's journey in business is unique. We each have our own stride, our individual pace, and our distinct path to success. It's a lesson that can profoundly impact our perception of ourselves and our businesses. Yes, others might have businesses that grew much faster than yours. But you don't know their full story. Maybe they left their old job and took a handful of clients with them to kick start their own business? Or perhaps they sacrificed every waking minute to work on their company? I know business owners who have lost partners, families, friends, and health in the pursuit of success.

I remember one business coach telling me "that hour you spend each evening watching Netflix with your wife, where would you be in ten years time if you spent that hour each night working on your business instead?"

"Divorced, burnt out, lonely and depressed" I replied. I understand the teaching, and if business success in a short a time as possible is all you want in life, then it's a powerful idea. But it didn't suit my pace, and that's fine.

Comparing yourself to others can be demoralising and counterproductive. Instead of obsessing over others' successes, embrace your own journey. Recognise that your path is uniquely yours, shaped by your experiences, skills, and circumstances. It's essential to set your own pace and to appreciate the progress you've made, no matter how incremental it may seem.

Success in business isn't about being the best or the fastest; it's about continuous improvement and personal growth. Or 'Kaizen' as the Japanese call it. You don't need to be the best; you only need to be better than you were yesterday. It's about setting your goals and striving to reach them, regardless of the benchmarks set by others.

The mountains teach us the importance of patience, resilience, and determination. They remind us that the journey itself is as important as the destination. In business, these lessons translate into the resilience needed to weather storms, the patience to build something meaningful over time, and the determination to keep moving forward.

As a business owner, your success is not defined by how you stack up against others, but by your ability to stay true to your vision and purpose. Your business is a reflection of your journey, your values, and your commitment. It's about embracing your own stride, finding your unique path, and staying focused on the goals that matter to you.

That last part is critical, because how you measure success will be different from other peoples. Sometimes I see other business owners arrive in a flash new Porsche or wearing a £15k Rolex, and I do feel a pang of envy that I don't have these things. But then I remember that these weren't my goals. My goals were to have freedom and flexibility, enough money not to struggle in life, be able to travel regularly, and to be able to give my wife a salary so that she can go part time in her job which gives us a lot of quality time together as a couple. And I've achieved that. What I want from life may not look as stylish as what others want in life, but to me it's the benchmark of success. Defining what success looks like for you is everything, and I believe finding your own pace and measure of success will lead to far greater happiness in the long term compared to "keeping up with the entrepreneurial Joneses" as it were.

So, as you navigate the terrain of business, remember the mountains' timeless lesson: go at your own pace, embrace your journey, and measure your success not by external comparisons but by the progress you make each day. The mountains remind us that success is a personal journey, and the summit is just one part of the adventure.

Actions

1. Set Your Own Goals and Measure Progress: Define your business objectives based on your unique vision and values. Set realistic goals and track your progress over time using relevant metrics and KPIs.

2. Embrace Your Unique Journey and Pace: Avoid comparing your business to others and recognise that everyone's path to success is different. Focus on your strengths, stay true to your values, and be patient with your business's growth.

22

The Art Of Delegation: The Power of a Well-Organised Team

Hiking the Inca Trail in Peru had been on my bucket list since I first saw pictures of Machu Picchu as a kid. When I finally found time to undertake the hike in 2015, one of the most memorable lessons I learned was the art of effective team work and delegation.

Our group set off on the four-day expedition with excitement and anticipation, keen to discover the rugged terrain and reach the legendary Machu Picchu. However, it wasn't long before we realised that the challenging feat of trekking through this magnificent landscape was only made possible by the incredible efforts of the local porters who accompanied us.

These porters, who acted with the precision of an elite military unit, were the unsung heroes of our expedition. Their impeccable organisation and division of labour were a sight to behold. It was a lesson in efficiency that every leader should heed.

One of my burning questions for the guide was how was it we were able to keep food, in particular meat, fresh for four days without power or refrigeration. The guide explained how the fastest porter, the sprinter of the group, would get up at the crack of dawn and run to the next camp site (*how anyone could run on a trail that we found physically exhausting to walk is beyond me!*) He would rush ahead to secure our campsite and stash our food in a cool spot before it spoiled, such as a river or a cool shady spot. This strategic move ensured that our supplies stayed fresh and safe from the heat of the day.

Then came the porters responsible for carrying the tents. With swift precision, they would pack away our tents after we had left each morning, overtake us on the walk, and ensure that by the time we arrived at the next camp our tents were all set up and waiting for us, allowing us to flop down, kick off our shoes and relax for a while before dinner.

The chef carried the stove, and was in charge of feeding the group. He would prepare hot, nourishing meals that seemed almost magical considering our remote location (*and even somehow baked a cake for us up in the mountains on our last day!*) That man cooked up better meals in a tent using a camping stove than I can in a fully furnished kitchen!

And let's not forget the incredible porters in charge of supplies. They carried our gear and equipment, making sure that we had everything we needed to tackle the trail from clean water to medical supplies. Without them, we'd have had to carry all our own gear, which would have made the already difficult trek impossible.

Our two guides, the leaders of our expedition, played critical roles as well. The lead guide, Alejandro, set the pace for the group, ensuring that we made steady progress without overexerting ourselves, as well as motivating us and keeping the mood high with his light-hearted humour and constant jokes.

The second guide stayed at the back of the group with the slowest walkers. His presence was reassuring, offering support and encouragement to those who needed it the most. He ensured that no one was left behind, emphasising that we were a team bound by a common goal.

Reflecting on this experience, I saw the immense importance of embracing delegation as a strategic tool rather than trying to do everything yourself (*as I so often had done*), and the true power of building an elite unit within your business. By distributing tasks and responsibilities among a skilled team, you can overcome challenges, reach new heights, and achieve success that may have seemed impossible to attain on your own.

In Business

One of the most influential business books I ever read was Michael E. Gerber's book "The E-Myth Revisited." This concept illustrates the importance of working on your business, not just in it, and it aligns perfectly with the lessons I learned on the Inca Trail, where delegation was key to our success.

The E-Myth is a story of three personas that exist within every business owner: the Entrepreneur, the Manager, and the Technician. The Entrepreneur is the visionary, the one who dreams big and sets the course for the business. The Manager is the organiser, responsible for creating systems and processes to keep things running smoothly. The Technician is the doer, the one who performs the hands-on work required to deliver products or services.

Much like the division of labour among the porters on the Inca Trail, these roles must be delegated effectively within a business to ensure success and sustainability.

On our Inca Trail journey, the Entrepreneur was akin to the lead guide who set the vision and goals for our expedition. Business owners must embrace their inner Entrepreneur, crafting a compelling vision for their company's future and defining the path to success. This role involves strategic planning, innovation, and the ability to see the bigger picture.

The Manager on the Inca Trail was represented by the porter responsible for organising camp and supplies. In business, this role is responsible for creating and maintaining the systems and processes that enable the company to function efficiently. Managers ensure that the day-to-day operations run smoothly, resources are allocated effectively, and goals are met.

The Technician in business is responsible for delivering the core product or service. Delegating this role allows business owners to avoid becoming trapped in the day-to-day grind and to focus on the bigger picture. Technicians are essential, as a business owner you should not be doing this yourself.

To build a successful business, entrepreneurs must balance these three personas and delegate effectively. Just as on the Inca Trail, where each porter had a specialised role, business owners should assemble a team with the right mix of skills and talents to support each aspect of the E-Myth.

Delegation is not merely about assigning tasks; it's about entrusting others with responsibilities, empowering them to make decisions, and creating a sense of ownership. I think it's critical that business leaders should foster a culture of mentorship and growth within their teams.

You cannot build a successful business if you insist on doing everything yourself, or you'll find you very quickly become the bottleneck in your own business. Hire skilled people who are better than you, then get out of their way. Your job is to grow the business and ensure everyone else does their job properly, not do their jobs for them. Without effective delegation, you'll find you hit a ceiling quite quickly in your business growth.

Action Points

1. Identify Your Entrepreneurial Vision: Take the time to define your long-term vision for your business. Set clear and inspiring goals that align with this vision. Consider what success means to you and your organisation.

2. Build a Delegation Plan: Identify tasks and responsibilities within your business that align with the Entrepreneur, Manager, and Technician roles. Determine which tasks are best suited for delegation and which require your personal attention. Develop job descriptions or role profiles for key positions within your team.

3. Assemble a Capable Team: Recruit team members with skills and strengths that complement your own. Prioritise hiring individuals who can excel in the Manager and Technician roles, allowing you to focus on the Entrepreneurial aspects. Invest in training and development to empower your team and enhance their capabilities.

4. Implement Efficient Systems and Processes: Work with your

Managerial team members to create efficient systems and processes that streamline operations. Document workflows and procedures to ensure consistency and scalability. Regularly review and refine these systems to adapt to changing business needs.

5. Promote a Culture of Ownership and Accountability: Encourage team members to take ownership of their roles and responsibilities. Foster an environment where individuals feel empowered to make decisions and contribute to the company's success. Set clear performance expectations and hold team members accountable for results.

6. Provide Mentorship and Guidance: Support team members in their development by providing mentorship and opportunities for growth. Offer constructive feedback and encourage continuous learning. Recognise and reward achievements to motivate and retain talent.

By implementing these action points, you can leverage the lessons from the mountains and "The E-Myth" to build a well-organised team, optimise your delegation strategies, and position your business for sustainable growth and success.

Our guide, Alejandro, leading us along the Inca Trail, Peru

23

The Twists and Turns on the Path to the Summit

In the world of mountaineering, as in life, the journey to the summit is rarely linear. It's a winding, unpredictable path, marked by twists and turns that challenge your resolve and test your mental strength. Let me take you on a journey through the rugged volcanic terrain in New Zealand, where I learned this valuable lesson first-hand.

We decided to embark on the legendary Tongariro Crossing, a 20km hike in New Zealand which involves traversing steep volcanic terrain. My then-girlfriend-now-wife and I were well prepared, stocked up with water, sandwiches and snacks, and a shared determination to complete our challenge.

As we began our ascent to the summit at Red Crater (1,886m), the path was clear, and our spirits were high. We climbed steadily, marveling at the breath-taking scenery around us. The sun was shining, the sky was blue, and our pace was strong.

But then without warning, the winds changed and the weather turned.

Dark clouds rolled in, obscuring our view and bringing a biting chill. Rain began to fall, the wind picked up, and our progress slumped. We huddled together and pushed forward, inch by inch. The summit was still our goal, but the lovely peaceful trek we had imagined in the warm New Zealand sun was gone.

As we ascended further, we encountered hidden valleys that we had to traverse, steep ascents, and difficult terrain covered in loose ash which made climbing difficult. As we got closer to the crater which was basically a big old pile of ash, I swear for every two steps forward we took we'd slide one step back.

But here's the beauty of mountaineering, and indeed, of life's challenges: sometimes it's a case of the harder the journey, the more satisfying the reward. We discovered our own inner strength and determination as a couple, and shared in the united joy of overcoming a tough struggle together.

Reflecting on the trek, I concluded that whilst the path to the summit may not always be linear, it is the journey itself that will shape you into the resilient, capable, and determined individual you need to be to achieve your goals. After all, if it was easy, everyone would do it. And what fun would that be?

In Business

In the world of business, the journey to success is rarely a straightforward path. It's more like an unpredictable mountain path filled with twists, turns, and unexpected detours. As entrepreneurs and leaders, we often set out with a clear vision and a well-thought-out strategy, but the reality of the business world is that it rarely adheres to our neatly laid out plans.

At the outset of starting a new business, we often hold onto the illusion of linearity. We envision a clear, upward trajectory where hard work and determination alone will carry us steadily toward our goals, imagining a straight line from Point A (our humble beginnings) to Point B (the pinnacle of success). We land a couple of big clients, smash last year's turnover, grow the team, and move into fancy new offices. "Yes, we're becoming successful!" we tell ourselves.

However, I've found it's often just when we think we've found our footing that an unexpected market shift or technological disruption can send us veering off course. Whether it's GDPR, Brexit, Covid or a recession, these external events can seriously derail our progress and throw us off track. There have been so many times when I've been in a place where I've said something like "we just need one more client to be in a great place financially" only to lose two or three clients in short succession, or just when I've thought we were about to have our most profitable quarter ever, a massive unexpected expense comes up that completely screws up our progress.

Consider the story of Uber, a once small start-up that set out to revolutionise the taxi industry by developing a mobile app for on-demand rides. Their initial vision was simple: connect riders with nearby drivers at the push of a button. They encountered numerous roadblocks along the way, from unexpected regulatory battles to fierce competition. They faced massive resistance from all directions. Yet, in the midst of these challenges, they stumbled upon the idea of expanding their services to include food delivery. This unexpected pivot turned them into a global tech giant, changing the way people access transportation and food. Today they're worth $139 billion.

I find that business success is like health or fitness - it is a temporary state; sometimes you have it, sometimes you don't. Successful entrepreneurs and companies understand the importance of being flexible and open to change. They recognise that their initial plans are not set in stone but are, instead, guidelines that need constant adjustment.

It's essential business owners acknowledge that the path to success is rarely a linear one. It's a complex and unpredictable journey filled with unexpected challenges and opportunities. Rather than being discouraged by the twists and turns, we must learn to embrace them, for it is in these moments of uncertainty that true innovation and growth often thrive.

Action Points

1. Embrace Adaptability:

- Make adaptability a core value in your business or personal approach to entrepreneurship. Encourage your team to be open to change and willing to pivot when necessary.
- Recognise that business success often depends on your ability to adapt to changing circumstances. Be proactive in seeking out new opportunities, even if they veer away from your initial plan. Foster a culture that values agility and embraces change as a means of growth.

2. Cultivate Chance:

- Create opportunities for positive chance by networking, attending industry events, and engaging with your local community. Stay open to unexpected encounters and collaborations.

- Serendipitous moments can be game-changers in business. By actively seeking out new connections and experiences, you increase the likelihood of stumbling upon valuable opportunities and insights that you might never have anticipated. Foster an environment that encourages and celebrates the potential of serendipity.

3. **Continuously Learn and Adapt:**

- Establish a system for ongoing learning and adaptation within your business or personal development. Regularly review and update your strategies, goals, and skill sets based on new insights and changing circumstances.
- In a non-linear path to success, the ability to learn from both successes and setbacks is crucial. Continuously gathering data, seeking feedback, and adapting your approach will help you stay ahead of the curve and make informed decisions.

The Tongoriro Crossing, New Zealand

24

Great communication makes for a great leader

One of the best guides I ever had was a man named Passang Tashi Sherpa who led us through the Nepalese Himalayas in 2017. He would start each morning with a daily briefing, advising us of the days' plans, weather forecasts, what we'd need to pack, and what we could expect from the day.

At the end of each day after dinner, he'd run through a team debrief. He'd see how we were all doing, congratulate us on the day's achievements, give us a brief overview of tomorrow's plans, and finally run through three simple questions:

1. What went well today?
2. What didn't go so well today?
3. What do we need to do differently tomorrow?

Question one was a great little morale booster to keep our spirits high. "Well done guys, today was tough, but you all did really well. You all seem to be coping ok with the altitude, and no one fell off that sketchy pass back there which is always an added bonus."

Next he'd say "so, come on guys tell me, is there anything that didn't go so well today?"

"I was struggling a little with all the dust" said one lady, "It gave me a nose bleed and I kept coughing."

"Ah yes very dusty. Dust bad." said Passang, "Make sure you wear a buff or scarf tomorrow to protect you from dust."

Each night we'd do this quick debrief, and each day as a team we came up with ideas to mitigate the various problems and challenges we were facing.

As I was getting ready to bed down for the night that first evening, Passang knocked on my door and said "Mr Joe, how you are doing?"

"Yes all fine" I replied.

"Very good very good. No aches or pains, no troubles?"

"Nope" I smiled, "All good!"

"Ok" he said, "Now tell me one thing that is going well, and one thing that could be better. And I will do the same."

Hmmm. That threw me! I thought about it for a minute.

"Well, I guess my fitness levels feel good. I'm not struggling with the pace and I'm coping fine. I suppose my knee could be better – the one with the torn ACL, it's been aching quite a bit. But that's normal, it always aches when I climb!"

Why had I kept quiet about my knee aching? Perhaps I was embarrassed. Perhaps I didn't want him to think I was weak. Perhaps I was concerned he'd pull me from the trek. Perhaps I'd just made my peace with it aching and concluded there was nothing anyone could do to help. Maybe I was just being British. Or possibly it was a combination of all of those things. Opening up about weaknesses rarely comes naturally.

"Ok" he said, "Thank you for letting me know. I'd agree with you, I think your fitness and strength is good. But I think you are a bit too fast on the descents and trying too hard to match pace with some of the others. You don't have to always keep up with them, they know you're just as fit as they are. But they don't have a damaged knee like you do. Take some ibuprofen before bed and again before you start trekking tomorrow. If the pain gets worse let me know ok?"

"Ok, thank you." I said. His suggestions helped. Each night he'd check on everyone in the team using this format. We came to expect it, so we knew that opening up wouldn't be awkward or bad. And he always had suggestions that helped. Just feeling you didn't have to suffer in silence helped.

I found his leadership style very reassuring and comforting, and it made me feel that I was always in safe caring hands that would help me through the challenge of the expedition.

In Business

I have never considered myself much of a natural leader, and always struggled with people management. I started my company as a shy introverted geek who was good at building websites and not very good at having frank conversations. However, as my team and business grew, my management abilities were forced to grow with it.

I thought about Passang's leadership style many times over the years. His simple approach seemed easy to apply and replicate with my team, and the consistency of the conversations meant they weren't awkward once we knew what to expect.

I have adopted his approach into my business, and the results have been game changing! Each week on a Monday morning, we start with a team briefing, looking at where we are with projects, who's going to be doing what, and any issues that need addressing.

At the end of each week we have a weekly de-brief, looking at what went well this week, what didn't go so well, and what new systems we need to implement.

Each quarter I have a 1-2-1 with everyone on my team. This is not a performance review, but a casual conversation out of the office where I ask what they feel is going well and what they feel isn't going so well. I do the same. This is a great way to encourage them to open up, build trust, and inspire open and honest communication. They know what to expect and come ready prepared with answers. And if there's ever an issue I need to address with somebody, it's not awkward having the conversation, because they're all very used to having 1-2-1s with me regularly. At the end of each year we do a structured formal review, where we look at the year just gone and a development path for the year ahead.

Adopting Passang's approach has allowed me to build much more of a positive rapport with my team, deal with problems quickly and efficiently, and win their respect as a leader.

Afterall, they say people don't leave companies, they leave bosses....

Action Points

1. **Weekly team meetings**
   If you're not already, start holding weekly team meetings on a Monday morning to assess where everyone is with various projects and tasks. Identify any challenges anyone is having. If you have a big team, you may wish to do this only with your senior leadership team. We used to call them **LION** meetings, which stands for *"Last week's Issues, Opportunities for Next week."*

2. **End of week de-briefs**
   Hold a quick de-brief with your team at the end of each week. Keep this short, and ask "This week - what went well, what didn't go so well, what new systems do we need to implement next week?"

3. **Quarterly reviews**
   With either your whole team or your senior leadership team, start scheduling regular informal reviews. Ask them "Tell me what do you're doing great at, and what do you feel you could improve on. I'll do the same."

4. **Annual reviews**
   Hold annual reviews with your team where you review the 12 months just gone, and put in place a development plan for the year ahead. You want to explore strengths, key accomplishments, areas

for improvement, plans to get things on track, and any additional changes or ideas.

Our guide Passang Sherpa, Himalayas, Nepal

25

A picture speaks a thousand words

There is no denying that a mountain expedition is tough – some of the toughest things I have done in my life. Often the toughness of it can taint my memories of a trip. People ask me when I get back how it was, and it would be easy to reply with "well, very tough. It was physically exhausting, the food sucked, I didn't sleep for five days, I was in pain the whole time, I felt sick as a dog from the altitude, I didn't get to shower in a week, and I felt cold like I've never felt cold before."

I think if it wasn't for the photos I take on my trips, that could very easily be my takeaway from some of these expeditions. However, often it is only when I look back at the photos that the true magic and wonder of the incredible scenery I've just seen comes back to me, and I remember just how fantastic an adventure the whole thing was.

"Wow, these look like shots from a movie! I can't believe you saw that! What an incredible adventure you've had" my friends would say when I showed them the pictures. And they were right! They are incredible adventures, and I do get to see some truly unbelievable things. But if it wasn't for the photos, I may never remember those. My memories would be of pain and suffering, and I might forget all the wonderful sights I had witnessed.

This is why I make an effort to always take as many photos as possible on my trips, so that I may look back and remember how truly magnificent my adventure was.

In Business

As 2023 drew to a close, I was sat in my coach's office reviewing the year just gone.

"So tell me about 2023 Joe. How do you think it went?"

"Pretty poor" I sulked. "We signed up 50% less clients than we did in 2022, I seemed to work harder than ever, we lost more retainer clients than we signed up, and I feel like we have gone backwards."

"Interesting," said my coach. "Let's review some of the wins. Tell me about your team size now vs last year?"

"Well we now have a second full time SEO technician, a full time support technician, and a full time junior designer. So we've grown by + three people."

"Ok, and what about your office?" he said.

"Well, this time last year we were in our old office and at capacity. We've now moved to a bigger office, we still have room for two more staff, plus we have our own boardroom to bring clients into, a separate kitchen area, upgraded iMacs for the whole team, a fancy new coffee machine, and a fresh water dispenser."

"And what about turnover?" he said.

"Well actually turnover is over £100k higher than last year, despite signing less clients. I suppose the contracts we've signed are bigger."

"And what about your work life balance?"

"Well, I suppose I was able to take three weeks off for my honeymoon and didn't have to respond to a single call, email or support ticket. I couldn't have done that a year ago!"

"And what about your systems and services?" he asked.

"Well, we've got a lot more systems in place, meaning things run far more smoothly and the team are less dependent on me. This year we've introduced App development, AI chatbots, and much more advanced web development thanks to some new tools. Oh, and I brought my first book out which is selling quite well on Amazon." I said.

"And what about your clients?" he said.

"Well we've signed a couple of big clients that most people would have heard of this year, and a couple of significant high profile clients in our local area that everyone knows about" I replied.

"Right. Still think it's been a poor year?" he said with a smirk on his face.

I concluded it had not. Just like in the mountains, I had forgotten all of the fantastic wins we had had this year, and was focussing on the negatives. Without my coach to remind me of the highlights, or "hypothetical photos," I would easily have slipped into a pit of despair and negativity, which is always a dangerous place to be as a company owner and team leader.

Action Points

Without photos or reminders of the highlights, it's easy to forget about the wins, and focus only on the negatives.

Make a new document called "current business status" and save it somewhere safe. Add the following to your list:

- Team size
- Turnover
- Profit
- Office
- Key clients
- Work life balance
- Time spent working on the business rather than in it
- Any other metrics you feel are relevant to your business to measure

Set a reminder in your calendar for one year's time to review your list (and add a note to your calendar entry reminding you where you saved it!) When your reminder goes off in a years time, review where you are compared to the "snapshot" you took of your company one year previously.

Spectacular views of Machu Picchu!

Shots like this in the Italian Alps remind you of the great adventures you had!

26

Keep to the path

When you have a set destination in mind (e.g. a mountain summit), it's of course critical you stick to the course you're on to get there safely and efficiently. If you hypothetically had unlimited time, resources and lives, then you could wander off to do all the exploring you want. But deviating from your designated route can be deadly in the mountains.

Firstly there's the time issue. Typically you'll want to be at your destination well before nightfall, when navigating is difficult, hazards are hard to spot, and freezing temperatures set in (plus if you arrive late to your hut, there's a good chance the chef will have finished for the day, meaning you go without an evening meal. Trust me I've been there! A chocolate bar for dinner after a hard day's trekking isn't fun!)

Then there's the resource issue. You'll usually only be carrying enough previsions to last for the amount of time you're planning to be out. If you took a detour to climb another peak or explore an interesting valley, you could well find yourself out of food and water before you've made it to your evening camp.

There's also the increased energy you'll burn exploring... if you've got a 12 hour hike ahead and you follow an interesting deviation which adds 4 hours to your route, you may well find you're completely exhausted by the time you finally reach your intended destination. And decisions made whilst exhausted usually aren't great! A great example of this was on the Everest Base Camp trek I did. On the first day of descent after reaching base camp, roughly half the group opted to do an additional trek up to Kala Patar, which should have taken around 3 hours with an extra 410m of ascent. I was tired and struggling with the altitude and nausea, so gave it a miss. The group that went up hit unexpected bad weather on the way down, which made their total diversion around 6 hours. Many of those who went up to Kala Patar really struggled with the additional 9 hour trek down to Pangboche due to exhaustion and fatigue. I'm glad I gave it a miss!

Finally there's unforeseen dangers. No mountain path is without risk, but wandering off down an unknown path where few have ventured could lead you wandering straight onto an unstable cliff or loose avalanche slope that you weren't prepared for.

Whilst quick detours to check out a stunning vista are mostly acceptable, it's imperative that any major detours are avoided at all costs.

In Business

Ah, distractions. Or "shiny object syndrome" – I see this so often with business owners! Many business owners are creative, entrepreneurial "ideas" people, and they go from one business idea to the next. I can't tell you how many business owners have come to us wanting a new website and brand created for their latest "gamechanger" of a business idea, only to close it down a few months later. If only they'd put all that energy and excitement into working on their existing business that was already doing well.

Trust me I get it, I've been there. I've neglected my existing business that was already doing well because I got excited by some new idea or technology, only to end up scrapping it later down the line to focus on the core offering that was already performing. Why? Probably because new is exciting. New ideas, seeing a brand come to life, an awesome vision – that's exciting! Refining systems, firefighting, dealing with petty issues, chasing late payments – that's dull. Really dull.

However, dull as it may be, if the mountains have taught me anything, it's that all deviations do is distract you and ultimately get in the way of progress. They can be expensive, dangerous, sap your energy, and harm your existing business. Sure, once you've arrived at your destination, by all means go for a little wander to see what else is around. But until you get there, stick to the path you're on and don't let anything divert your focus.

I've found that in both the mountains and in business, success isn't normally achieved by those with any particular skill or talent; it's achieved by those who knew their path and stuck to it. They plodded on and on and on, one foot after another, refusing to give up, until they made it.

Actions

1. If, like me, you're easily excited by new ideas, then place a jar on your desk with a label that says "ideas jar." Whenever you have an awesome idea, write it down and stick it in your jar. DO NOT impulsively jump on the idea the second you have it. You're in

a heightened state of excitement and enthusiasm, and emotion will cloud your logical judgment. At the end of each month, decide which ideas from your jar you'll scrap, and which you'll discuss with your team / partner / business coach. If the idea is truly that good, it will still be relevant in a few weeks time. I often find that by the time the excitement has passed, suddenly it doesn't seem like such a great idea anymore.

2. Write out clear 12 month goals, and then further break this down into quarterly goals and 90 day plans. This will give you a clear journey and path to follow and help you avoid the inevitable shiny new objects that will no doubt present themselves.

3. Write out how you'll reward yourself when you hit each goal (a holiday with the family, a new watch, a new car etc.) This fantastic, highly motivating reward that you've promised yourself should excite you more than the idea of the shiny object, helping keep you on the path of focus and determination.

27

Type Two Fun

Mountaineers often describe their time in the mountains as "type two fun." By that, we mean that it's often not very fun doing it, but only when you look back afterwards that you realise what a fantastic adventure you had.

There are many times in the mountains where I've been battered by rain / hail / wind, shivered myself to sleep, felt sick to my stomach from altitude sickness, and wanted nothing more than to go home and curl up in my warm, dry, comfortable house.

So why do I keep doing it again and again? Because when I look back, I forget about the pain and discomfort. I remember the incredible sights I saw and the moments that took my breath away, like sipping a cold beer at sunset outside a mountain cabin or waking up to find a sea of clouds hanging below us, and the laughs I had with friends. I remember conquering the challenges, pushing myself mentally and physically harder than I thought possible, and finding strength within me that I didn't know I had. I remember the scary times where I stared death in the face and was lucky to come out the other side – the things that make you feel truly alive! The travel, adventure, cultures and people you encounter on your journeys change you, and give you a different perspective on the world.

I'd do it all again in a heartbeat, and wouldn't change any of it. Sometimes the temporary hardship and discomfort is worth it for the end accomplishment.

In Business

There are many examples of Type two fun I've encountered in business. Things that seem dull and painful at the time, but lead to greater reward later.

Hiring new employees is an example of this. The act of finding, recruiting, hiring, training and then paying for a new member of staff is always painful for small businesses, especially when they're first starting out. I remember the days of taking on my first staff, how frustrating it was spending ages explaining something to them, and then watching them spend ages doing it and making mistakes knowing I could probably do it myself in ten minutes.

Or writing systems... trying to write and document systems and processes that are in my head based on decades of experience is probably one of the dullest tasks I can think of in business (for me anyway, some love it!)

In the mountains with Type two Fun, you're exchanging pain for memories. Pain and discomfort are your currency, and memories and adventures are what you're purchasing. In business, time and money are your currency, and more time than you initially had, less problems, an empowered team, and enhanced scalability are what you get back. Spending time and money on hiring and training a new employee is what you put in; what you get back is the ability to take on more projects, scale the business, and ultimately take a holiday without having to work through it or all work coming to a standstill.

Now whenever I have a painful task to do, I sit and ask myself what the reward will be at the end of it. What will this discomfort bring me later down the line? It's a bit like ensuring your Christmas lights are neatly wound up before you pack them back in the box in January; it's a chore at the time, but will make your life so much easier next year when you're putting up the tree and don't have to bother untangling a mess of lights!

Actions

1. Write a list of ten things you absolutely hate doing in business
2. Write out a document containing information on how you can eliminate these tasks (*e.g. delegate them, hire someone to do them, automate them, eliminate the need for them all together*).
3. Now write a list of all the pain points associated with eliminating these tasks (*if there was no pain, you'd have eliminated them already!*)
4. Finally, write a list of the gains / rewards you'll get once they're gone (*more time, more work satisfaction, get to focus on more important business tasks etc*).

28

Take in the views

"Let's take a break" I suggested to my wife, on our ascent of a peak who's name I can't recall in the Canadian Rockies.

"We're nearly there" she panted, "let's keep going."

So we compromised and kept going. We pushed on to the top, before finally slumping down and laying in the cool breeze at the summit, exhausted and struggling to catch our breath. We'd made it to our destination, but the climb had been long and tough, and broken us.

If reaching the destination is your only goal then there's nothing wrong with this approach, and sometimes when you have a long climb and are racing against the clock it's critical. But personally I like to stop, take breaks, take in the views, and enjoy the journey. I want to look back and remember the experience as a positive one, not just an arduous challenge.

I believe it's important to find happiness in the moment, not just when you hit your goal. If you always postpone your happiness by tying it in with a future event, e.g. "I will be happy when I achieve this goal," then you don't enjoy the journey and you don't find happiness in the now. I try to celebrate the little wins along the way, such as "when I get to that rock I'll have a bit of chocolate" or "I'm going to stop for 5 minutes at that ridge up there and admire my progress."

I think it's nice to find happiness at every opportunity along the way, and celebrate the little wins as well as the big achievement. This way, you're not just celebrating the big win at the end and postponing your happiness, but you're enjoying the journey and celebrating the little wins along the way.

In Business

Success in business is often a result of meticulous goal setting, hard work and dedication. When I first started doing goal setting, I used to focus everything on hitting those big goals. I'd set big goals with big rewards, i.e. "when we hit this turnover I'll treat myself to a new watch" or "once we've signed 10 clients I'll book a holiday for my wife and I."

I found that whilst these big rewards were highly motivating, it also meant the journey sucked. I was working flat out, stressed, exhausted, and postponing being happy. I felt I couldn't rest or couldn't be happy until I had hit the big goal I was aiming for, those Big Hairy Audacious Goals that motivational speakers always tell us to aim for.

It was only when I started celebrating the little wins as well as the big ones that I really started to enjoy the journey. For example, I'd say "when we sign 2 clients I'll take my wife out for a nice dinner" or "when we hit 25% of our turnover target I'll treat the team to a work night out." For micro wins I'd crack open a bottle of Prosecco with the team, or bring in a home made cake.

I was staying on track and not losing focus or getting distracted, but it meant I was having fun along the way and enjoying the journey, celebrating the progress as well as the result. I found I was enjoying the day-to-day grind much more, and each mini milestone felt much more achievable than the stretch goal set for the end of the year.

Plus, sometimes your stretch goal can feel impossible. Celebrating the progress along the way can be a great way of reminding you how far you've come.

Actions

Hopefully by now you're in the habit of setting annual, quarterly and weekly goals.

1. Write down big rewards for hitting your big goals, medium rewards for your quarterly goals, and mini rewards for your weekly goals. These can be whatever you want – from a holiday with the family or a new car, to treating yourself to a new book or a hot bath.

2. Print pictures of these rewards and stick them next to each weekly, quarterly and 12 month goal plan. I always find having pictures helps motivate me and make the vision more real.

3. Finally, remember to have fun and enjoy the journey!

29

Energy is key

One of the most important aspects of a mountain expedition is without a doubt energy. Without energy you won't last long and won't get very far. Your body is burning calories at an increased rate over a prolonged period, and requires a good deal of sustained energy to be able to do this comfortably.

In order to have sustained energy for both performance and endurance, it's important climbers load up on the right kind of fuel. Too often I've seen climbers load up on sweets and sugar for a quick energy boost, only to crash hard and hit a wall a short time later. The right kind of food needs to be high in both calories and carbohydrates, whilst also being easy to digest – your stomach is less effective at high altitude, and your digestion doesn't work as well as it does normally (*I remember one climb in Peru where I decided eating a 2000 calorie meal replacement cookie was a good idea. Bad choice – I spent the rest of the trip feeling like I had a brick in my stomach!*)

A meal plan should be quite carefully researched and planned out. You need a good mix of both simple and complex carbs, protein, healthy fats, salts, and nutrients, all whilst keeping it lightweight, durable (*it needs to survive being out of the fridge for a few hours and getting bashed around in a backpack!*) and tasty (*when you've got no appetite at 5,000m and nausea is crippling but you know you need to eat, that home-made coconut and fig energy ball your partner baked might suddenly seem less appealing!*)

Getting your food and nutrition wrong not only means fatigue and exhaustion, but also leads to negative mindset. That nagging, whining little voice in your head starts piping in with "I knew this was a stupid idea, why am I here, I hate this, why can't we be down on the ground with a nice hot meal." And when that sets in, you're really in for a rough ride!

In Business

Like climbers, all businesses depend on energy to operate. And by energy, I mean money, which comes from customers, and customers come from leads. In order to have a steady stream of customers, we of course need a steady stream of leads coming into our business.

And yet, I see so many business owners who never really pay much attention to what is such a critical part of business. They sit and wait, hope for the best, or depend on word-of-mouth referrals. You would never set out on a mountain climb without food or water and just hope for the best, or hope that you'll get lucky and find some food up there. So why the hell would you start a business without a properly thought-out strategy for lead generation?

I can't tell you how many times I've spoken to business owners who have complained that they're quiet right now, and I ask what they're doing to generate leads and the answer is "nothing." On the mountains if you came across a climber who was struggling with fatigue, and you'd asked what they'd eaten, and they replied "nothing" you'd think "this guy's an idiot! What the hell's wrong with you!" Yet somehow in business this seems very commonplace!

It's essential that businesses have a structured plan for consistent lead generation. Consistent leads generate consistent customers which generates consistent cash flow. However, I often hear the following excuses when I raise this with business owners:

"We can't afford to spend any money on marketing or advertising."

"We don't know how."

"Well we didn't do any marketing last year and we were fine!"

"We spent some money on a campaign in the past and it didn't work, we just lost money."

"We don't have time to do it, we're always so busy."

Do any of those sound familiar? Let me address some of these, because if you run out of fuel, you'll end up crashing, hard. You'll end up stressed and exhausted, in a negative mindset, and struggling to run.

Just like how a climber should refuel before they run out of energy, you want to ensure you're working on your lead generation before you run out of current clients! You must find the budget for marketing, or if you have no budget you must dedicate the time to do it yourself. If you don't know how, either educate yourself or outsource it. Just because you didn't do marketing previously, it doesn't mean you don't need to do it now – markets change, competitors up their game, and trends come and go. If something failed in the past, that doesn't mean you shouldn't do marketing again, you just learn from your mistakes! I didn't stop eating after the meal replacement cookie incident, I just avoided eating one of those again.

Ultimately, you must dedicate the time and resources to making lead generation happen, consistently. If a climber does not stop to eat or hydrate because they're too busy climbing, they'll end up crashing hard when the energy runs out. Markets and consumer behaviour can change in an instant, and a dry sales pipeline will lead to struggles down the line.

Actions

1. If you're not actively tracking your leads, start doing so. You should always have a healthy pipeline of new leads, and when a pipeline starts going quiet, it gives you an early warning of problems down the line. I like visual pipeline tools like Pipedrive and Hubspot, which allow me to see in an instant how empty or full my sales funnel is looking.

2. Write down how many warm leads you need a month. I like to multiply the number of clients we need each month by three; if I want to land four new websites in a month, I'll need 12 good leads (*by a good lead, I mean someone who is looking to buy and can afford your services. If someone phoned us up and said they were starting a small business and had a budget of £150 for a website, we'd politely say no thank you and we wouldn't qualify them as a lead.*)

3. Now that you know how many leads you need each month, you

need to devise a strategy to actively generate this number. I like to split this into three different channels in order to avoid putting all my eggs in one basket. Different things work differently for different businesses, but for us it might look like:

- Organic SEO activities in our local area to generate 4 leads per month.

- Paid advertising outside of our local area to generate an additional 4 leads per month.

- A telemarketing campaign to our existing database to see if they have any needs, or know someone who does, to generate the final 4 leads per month.

I think the multichannel strategy is good because trying to generate 12 good leads from a single channel can be quite difficult, and can seem overwhelming. However, if the target is only four leads from that one channel, suddenly that seems much more realistic.

Often when I talk to business owners struggling with lead generation, they say something like "Well we're doing paid socials and that's going ok, generating about 4 leads a month, but it's still not enough."

"Ok great, keep doing that!" I'll say, "now we just need 2 more channels to get you to where you need to be!"

Finally, devise a system to actively track leads and where they came from. We need to learn what is working well for us and what isn't. If it's working well, we can do more of that. If it isn't, stop wasting time and money on it and move on to another channel.

30

Into the fog

I was once trekking with a team across the Aletsch Glacier, high in the Swiss Alps in 2012. It was a long trek, the weather was good, and the team were doing well.

Out of nowhere, a thick, dark cloud rolled over the mountain tops and down onto the glacier, smothering us in a dense fog. We stopped and roped up together for safety. I could just about see the person behind me if I looked back, but no further than that.

We trekked along, initially jovial. We'd all whistle tunes, call out jokes and banter with each other in the fog. However as the time went on, the morale stared to fade. On and on and on we trekked, with absolutely no let up in the fog. After several hours of seeing nothing but white, your mind starts playing tricks on you. You start thinking you can see shapes and outlines of peaks that aren't there. The glacier was vast, and you can literally walk for miles and miles across it without encountering anything.

I kept glancing at my compass in case it knew something that I didn't.

Sadly it did not. I was sure we should have been at our destination by now.

Five hours in and I started to despair. Were we lost? Had we actually all died and this was some strange after life place? Had we been going around in circles the whole time? We didn't have a GPS with us, and our maps were useless with no landmarks to cross-reference our position with.

I concluded that the only tool I had left in my belt was faith. Not a religious faith as such, but faith that we weren't lost, we were heading in the right direction, we hadn't in fact died, and we would eventually reach out destination. Faith was the only option I had, faith that we would be alright and everything would be ok.

Eventually, after what felt like a damn eternity, the mountain line and our destination cabin suddenly appeared metres in front of us, looming out of the fog like an iceberg appearing from the dark at sea. I felt like Noah sighting land for the first time, and let out a cry of joy!

Back on the glacier I had only two options: give up and accept my fate, or have faith that if we just kept going eventually we would reach our destination. I chose faith – the only real choice I had.

In Business

There have been several times in business that felt like it did back on that glacier; lost in the fog with no end in sight.

The pandemic and lock-down of 2020 was one example. Every company we spoke to had furloughed their staff, and every project we had on the cards was put on hold. There was literally nothing coming in. We were losing clients left, right and centre. Our costs were still pouring out. And there was no end in sight, no inclination as to when this financial hell would be over. I knew we had enough in our emergency funds to cover us for a good 3-4 months with no new business, but that still didn't stop me lying awake at 3am every morning stressing about the lack of cashflow with no way to fix it.

There's been other similar instances – times when something really bad happened that shook our stability and confidence to the core, and I had no idea when we'd see the end of it.

And every time I've had almost no control over the environmental, economic or external factors causing the panic. I have however had two choices: give up, or have faith we'll get through it and come out the other side.

Every time I've chosen faith. And you know what, 9 years in and we're still here. We've had some very tough times, but it's that blind faith, that burning desire to succeed, and a refusal to quit that sets apart the winners from the losers.

I've seen some really good agencies go under in the time I've been running mine – great agencies that had been around a long time and did some really fantastic work. The difference between us and them? They quit, we kept going. That's all! It wasn't down to savviness or skill or experience. Just dog-headed determination and a refusal to give up.

Right before the cloud came down! The Swiss Alps

This was our view for about 6 hours

31

Final Thoughts

I've learned many lessons up in the mountains, both through needing to think clearly under pressure and make life or death decisions, and through the time where I was able to think and reflect with no distractions or interruptions for hours on end.

Yes I have made mistakes on the mountains and in business, but what matters is I did learn from them, and I took on board the lessons I had learnt and took action to improve for next time.

If I can leave you with one final thought, it's this: take action. Struggling with something? Take action. Want to achieve something? Take action. Not happy? Take action.

You won't get it right all the time, no one does. But at least if you take action you won't stay where you are. And if the action you took didn't work, take more action! Do something different!

Action usually comes with risk; don't risk more than you can afford to lose. In business that's money, in the mountains that's your life.

But doing nothing also carries risk. Risk is inevitable, but without risk there's no reward.

Enjoy the journey, embrace the challenges, and most importantly, have fun!

G

www.ingramcontent.com/pod-product-compliance
Lightning Source LLC
Chambersburg PA
CBHW050101230526
45470CB00004B/1631